Value Mindset

Value Mindset

Accelerate Your Value Transformation by Changing Your Mindset

By Stephan M. Liozu, PhD

Value Innoruption Advisors Publishing • Sewickley PA • 2017

Value Mindset:
Accelerate Your Value Transformation by Changing Your Mindset
By Stephan M. Liozu, Ph.D.

Published by
Value Innoruption Advisors Publishing
PO Box 208
Sewickley, Pennsylvania 15143
www.valueinnoruption.com

ISBN: 978-1-945815-02-7 trade paperback
ISBN: 978-1-945815-03-4 ebook

First printing

Design and composition: www.dmargulis.com

MANUFACTURED IN THE UNITED STATES OF AMERICA

To my two loves: Lorenzo and Katie

Thank you for your support and your love,
and for inspiring me to be a better human being.

Contents

Acknowledgments

O VER THE PAST FIVE years, I've had the pleasure of working with many clients and of embarking on various value transformations around the world. These were enriching experiences at many levels. Now I'm leading a value transformation at Thales, and it's an equally fascinating project in a company that is helping to reshape the world and that stands at the forefront of technology. I am thankful to have been given all these opportunities. I am thankful for the ability to research and observe value transformations that are very successful and those that are less than successful. I am indebted to the people who took risks in transforming their organization's value mindset and who trusted my support and expertise. Thank you to all these brave leaders. You are a true inspiration to me.

This book is also the result of a long collaboration with my writing and design team. Iris Yann (irisyan1@gmail.com) designed all the visuals and comics. She is brilliant. Frank Luby injected his writing magic into the manuscript and provided a lot of energy during the project. He was an inspiration to get this done in just a few months. I would also like to thank Tommy Warburton for his support. Kristen Ebert-Wagner (editor@eberteditorial.com) and Dick Margulis (dick@dmargulis.com) made this project possible by providing tremendous support in editing, formatting, designing, and assembling the book. I thank this great team, and I look forward to many more projects in the future.

I hope you enjoy this book. I dedicate it to all the value heroes out there!

Value Mindset

Introduction

THINK ABOUT THE WORD "mindset" for a moment. How would you define it? Of course we could look up some clinical or dictionary definition for it, but such information usually offers little help for a business setting. You could also list a few things a mindset might encompass. When people used to ask me at the start of a business transformation, I would say something like this: mindset refers to the willingness of the individual and/or team to accept challenges, embrace change, and experiment with new concepts and techniques that will allow them to be more successful in work and in life.

Then I found a much better answer.

I learned, sometimes the hard way, and later in my career through better planning and awareness, that the most important factor in a successful business transformation is mindset. It's more important than any tool, any process, any training session, or any

single financial incentive. But you can't will a positive mindset into existence. No one can snap their fingers or hypnotize a team into believing in the mission, believing in the transformation, or ultimately believing in their team and in themselves.

What I also discovered in my coaching and consulting work for transformations is that almost anyone can learn to adopt a growth mindset, or what I will more specifically refer to as a value mindset. *Almost* is the key word. With the right programs, resources, and level of energy, you can get almost anyone on board. There is a way to cultivate these mindsets, and likewise a way to make that learning integral to planning and executing a business transformation.

That's what this slim, easy-to-read book is about. Of course it's an obligation in such a book to deliver the how-to parts. Yes, this book will impart the tools, steps, and insights necessary to enhance your level of customer value maturity and to transform your current approaches to ones that are vastly more successful, mostly because they are driven by the unstoppable tailwind of a value mindset.

At the same time, I also feel an obligation to make this process fun and to kindle an excitement for learning and exploring (two characteristics, by the way, of a value mindset). This is not learning for learning's sake. It is part of an attitude that makes continual learning necessary for business survival and, on a personal level, career survival. Many industries are undergoing unprecedented transformations. People argue that the ones who lose in these transformations are those who *cannot pivot and adapt*. But I put more faith in people's abilities, ambitions, and desires to help themselves and would turn that statement around. The winners in these transformations are those who are *willing to pivot and adapt*. Often, news and research focus on companies that cannot transform and thus disappear. But thousands succeed and make the required changes. That's the good news!

It begins, continues, and ends with a value mindset.

Over the next ten chapters I lay out the steps for fostering a value mindset, and for living that mantra. In those chapters I do my best to mix the *why* with the *how* and do so while keeping the story, and your journey, moving along.

The first two chapters lay the groundwork and give us a basic vocabulary to talk about customer value transformations (chapter 1) and that indispensable ingredient that defines their success or failure, the value mindset (chapter 2). In chapters 3 through 8, we talk about the most important aspects of a value mind-set one by one. These are the six As: attitude, action, ability, adaptability, alignment, and accountability.

"To change your life, you have to change yourself. To change yourself, you have to change your mindset."

Wilson Kanadi

In chapter 9, I describe best practices for training excellence, because training and communication are essential components of a value transformation and mindset change. This training is not what you are accustomed to, however. I advocate an end to one-way classroom teaching and advocate for a mix of newer, proven approaches that build engagement, reinforce the messages, and make a difference.

In chapter 10 you will find out how to get started. It's the question everyone asks once they understand the empowerment and energy that a value mindset imparts. They want it for the organization and also for themselves personally. This process can take years. I want to be upfront about that. Yet you have to start somewhere, and chapter 10 begins to draw that map.

For this book, I have adopted another style. You will notice lots of quotes and comics to support my main arguments and to illustrate some of the key concepts. All of these are original drawings produced for this book. In an age of design, I wanted to bring the required jazziness to make this read a fun one. I hope you enjoy them.

No need to introduce much more. Let us get into the meat of the value mindset!

1

What Is Customer Value Transformation?

GET READY TO CHANGE!

Those may be the scariest four words in the English language, at least for a business conversation at this stage of the 21st century. It's scary, because without details the phrase is ambiguous at best. What could it possibly mean?

Let me put your mind at ease.

At its broadest level, the type of change I focus on in this book is very specific. It is a customer value transformation. This puts the customer at the center of the business, precisely the way Peter Drucker meant it when he said "the purpose of business is to create and keep a customer."

If a business wants to do that, it must answer a few questions: What do our clients or customers hold dear? What keeps them up at night? What do they value, and how can we use those perceptions and desires to better engage them and offer them products and services they benefit from? These fundamental questions are the very basis for why we create companies and products.

We are here to create more value for each other.

The term *customer value* addresses what your clients and customers consider important. Buying your product involves more than just an exchange of money. Your customers have choices about what to buy and where to buy it, and what they value will guide how they make those choices. So it seems logical that the company that aligns itself with its customers, and that takes care to preserve that alignment, will prosper. To reach that prosperity in your organization, you will need to tailor your own particular actions to focus on what the customer values. That is what makes a customer value transformation necessary.

From the CEO to the line employee to the salesperson on the road, every individual will also undergo a transformation, because each needs his or her own customer focus. An enormous positive side effect is that ultimately everyone will be more motivated, more productive, and more satisfied with the company. They will be proud of where they work because they're serving customer needs. This attitude becomes a state of mind and penetrates deeply into the DNA of the organization. As a result, it will manifest itself in the company's top line and bottom line.

This is the essence of a value mindset.

The transformation you undertake will not happen overnight. It will occur through consistent training and retraining, through being open to new approaches, and through embracing the new tools you will receive. This transformation must permeate all levels of management, not only the rank and file, so that all levels of the company are aligned. The transformation will be both challenging and exhilarating. You're undertaking a journey, a journey with vast intrinsic and extrinsic rewards.

Please remember that the transformation in some form is unavoidable. The saying from the last chapter about learning as a competitive advantage rings in my ears the same way Peter Drucker's comment does. We need to make learning our habit and customers our mission.

Understanding the journey

Each customer value transformation is different. Putting customer value at the forefront of everything you do is a journey and a process. No two paths or methods are quite the same, just as no two people or companies are the same. This journey is influenced by the traveler, the choices available, and the decisions you make, such as the reward you seek for serving your customers so well and how you will define success. It also depends on where you begin and where you want to go. While transformations can take some time, you need a starting point and a general roadmap to make you see and appreciate the destination. In between, there might be peaks and valleys, like in any journey!

The journey of a customer value transformation has different steps, or mechanics if you will. The outset of the journey—the front end of the transformation—is all about putting the tools in place, the core or systemic values, the standardized approaches, and the aligned structure within the company. The transformation plan gains support as practices are adopted and people adapt. Value-focused actions are reinforced and slowly become habit.

It is at this point that you as a manager should be prudent. This is most often where a transformation breaks down. It might happen because of a lack of reinforcement or a lack of support from top management or from peers and co-workers. That is how this book's approach to a customer value transformation differs: we will delve into additional communication, additional coaching, and additional training on the use of tools throughout the journey. This will guide and support you to ensure the success of your transformation journey.

Later in the journey—toward the back end of the transformation—the commercial processes, pricing plans, and competitive responses will have been practiced and polished, but they are never perfected. They might not have been fully assimilated into the fabric of the organization. You always have room for improvement and refinement, but you will also have a unified group of people equipped with the tools, the system, the direction, and the strategy to get things done and hold themselves accountable.

> **Standards of a value transformation**
> ☑ **Champions are on board**.
> ☑ You have built some **internal capabilities**.
> ☑ You have designed **tools** and deployed **systems**.
> ☑ Your value management **process** is in place.
> ☑ Your **value experts** are "pumped up."
> ☑ Your **value propositions** and models are tested.

Anyone can begin a journey. Anyone can get the right tools, the super consultants, the best people, and the attention of the CEO. Many companies get started fast, do well, and then stall. It's hard work. It's more than a standard change management project or strategic initiative. So I'd like to help you not only finish it, but finish it with a level of success and change that may pleasantly surprise you. I want you to experience the level of flow that the value masters realize when they achieve their goals. The key difference between a good value transformation and a great one is the value mindset.

Stay focused and find your allies

Over the course of an arduous journey, people may come and go as they decide whether the trip appeals to them and the mission is worth the effort. It's inevitable that some won't like or accept the changes you're trying to implement. They may disrupt, they may impede progress, or they may leave.

This may be unfortunate, but it shouldn't cause you to second-guess your decisions. Doing so would send the wrong message to the people, probably the majority, who have made the effort and seen the merits of the transformation and a value mindset. I would urge you to replace those who depart with new people who have the right mindset, the right affinity for the culture, and a refreshing willingness to experiment. It will offer you a unique opportunity to find people with the right attitude and behavior.

You can't cherry-pick your way to success

Remember while reading this book and undertaking your transformation that this is the basis for a program that you design and implement. There are no shortcuts. Putting only one or two of the easier steps in place is not an option if you want to achieve a value transformation. The steps all work together to achieve the desired result. So, yes, it takes time to go through all the steps and successfully transform. But if you can adopt 100 percent of the ideas in this book, you can save two to three years on the typical value transformation, which can last up to six years. Adopting this mindset will offer intensity, an acceleration of change, and a higher quality of change.

Your reality will fall between 0 percent and 100 percent, but I hope you get as close to the higher number as possible. That will determine where you end up on the pricing capability grid. Simply put, pricing power is only possible with the combination of two things: value-based pricing backed by strong implementation. Having one without the other costs you money and may ultimately cost you customers and even the business. Value-based pricing without execution is like getting an A in a business school classroom. You've learned a lot, but you haven't done anything.

Execution without value-based pricing means that you're selling your customers, your products, and yourself short.

Doing both requires learning and commitment, and that third component many people may find elusive until they start learning more about it: the value mindset.

The shift from a pricing transformation to a value transformation encompasses so much. It accounts for

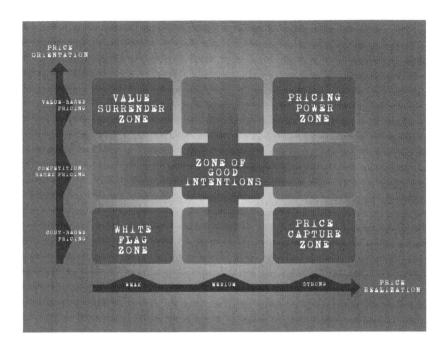

the different needs in a customer and a market, and it also aligns your organization. Value acts as a fluid in your organization. It gels and links the functions within your business, aligning everyday actions and moving everybody in the organization in one direction. It's also the glue that bonds your team and your actions together, creating the platform for success. The value mindset complements and reinforces your existing knowledge and talents, but with a shift in perspective.

The last thing you need is a technical and traditional pricing person leading a value transformation. It won't work. They may communicate the mechanics you need, but not the spirit that fuels the transformation. This might sound bold and controversial. I am often asked "Can a pricing manager lead a value transformation?" My answer is "It depends!" It depends on that person's leadership skills. It also depends on the organizational culture. In some organizations, pricing might have negative connotations. In that case, rename this function *value,* not pricing. Bottom line: a person with great leadership skills, charisma, political clout, and energy levels can lead this value transformation.

Preparing your transformation

Central to this idea is that a value mindset is not achieved and cultivated through a robotic set of responses for an individual to use. Providing anything akin to a set of robotic responses is undesirable. A value mindset in your organization confers a new form of intuition upon your team. It's hard to express this to people who may want everything spelled out in spreadsheet specifics, but at some point your organization reacts because they *know* what to do and how to do it. They don't have to look it up in a book or debate it endlessly. It's in their hearts, in their bloodstream, and ultimately in their DNA. Allowing people to embrace and explore these new processes is what will accelerate the transformation.

Even when everyone "gets it," they won't necessarily automatically act on what they've learned. The theory will be the easy part that every individual

"To successfully respond to the myriad of changes that shake the world, transformation into a new style of management is required. The route to take is what I call profound knowledge - knowledge of leadership of transformation."

William Edwards Deming

understands and agrees with; we can all concur that most organizations need to be more value-oriented. It's the sometimes difficult steps we must take to put these theories into practice that people will question.

Many approaches help here. You'll notice my referring frequently to a value journal or value log, which you can put to good use throughout the transformation. Each person will become accountable for taking actions and recording what they did, how they added value, how they helped a customer or a colleague that day. This will help build acceptance and make the new customer-centric approaches second nature.

When I talk of a value mindset, by no means do I refer to a panacea, a magic tonic that will infuse any business situation with a positive, cooperative, inspiring, and aspirational atmosphere. Most of the transformations I've undertaken involved helping a company realize its untapped potential or overcome its inertia in the face of greater competition or greater customer demands.

My colleagues who also do transformations tell me that the value mindset may meet some resistance in situations where the business faces an existential challenge. The urgency in those situations measures timelines in days and weeks, not months and years. While I do feel that the advice and insights in this book will help anyone looking to change a company or change themselves, the best fit for the value mindset is the company seeking lasting, long-term improvement, not imminent survival.

Make this a priority

Most large organizations, and many smaller ones, have too many priorities, too many conflicting objectives, and insufficient accountability—because even the most talented and gifted people can only serve so many masters well. One way to combat this overload is to conduct an alignment audit before embarking on this transformational journey. Begin by examining potential areas for misalignment, including objectives, incentives, communication, and engagement with customers and colleagues. This audit will identify places to start making improvements.

As we move forward, we will work with this audit and update it to show progress and whet our appetites for more. We will use it to integrate value into our organizations. Once integrated, everything still needs to be aligned. Your tools will help. You'll have the right attitude, know what actions you're going to take, and be trained on how to get things done. This alignment is at the heart of what we aim to do. Everything will transform, from the individual up through the organization and back down again. And at the core of creating this alignment is what will be discussed in the next chapter: the value mindset.

Key learning

_____

_____

_____

_____

Key actions

_____

_____

_____

_____

2

What Is a Value Mindset?

© LIOZU 2016

W̲ᴇ ʀᴇᴠᴇᴀʟ ᴏᴜʀ ᴍɪɴᴅꜱᴇᴛ in the actions, large and small, that we take each day. In our daily professional lives, it can be something as simple as working down a list of menial tasks or setting a modest goal for self-improvement.

Even with all the best tools and practices in place, your transformation won't succeed without the appropriate mindset. And exactly what is that mindset? It's the one that pushes you to extend and stretch yourself incrementally so you can get big gains from the cumulative effects of small improvements. It's what drives you to make ten sales calls or customer service calls instead of eight; then, a couple of weeks later, to make twelve or thirteen or fifteen. This is the mindset that prompts you to wake up one morning and ask "what was I doing with myself before this change?" The same thinking has underpinned conditioning programs such as weightlifting for decades: you set a tough target, do enough reps to make hitting that target easy, and then set the next target. After several months of executing that program, you're moving mountains.

Creating and nurturing that mindset takes time, effort, and training and coaching from skilled individuals, followed by reinforcement and encouragement from peers, and then ultimately your own inner drive. But in the end, it's worth it.

For your professional life, we call this a value mindset.

Open up to change

The value mindset builds on what Professor Carol Dweck calls the "growth mindset." She contrasts this with a fixed mindset, as shown in the chart below.

Here I ask you honestly: who would want to identify with the left side of the chart? The right side exudes energy and optimism. Imagine the potential that an organization can unlock and deliver when it thinks in terms of the growth mindset, not the fixed mindset.

A value mindset is a special kind of growth mindset, one that can drive the customer value transformation

Adopting Value to Grow and Learn

Fixed Mindset		Growth Mindset
I am good enough; status quo is good; cruising along	**Training and Skills**	Focus on learning and developing; eager to learn and experiment
Must be avoided; not willing to show vulnerability; sign of weakness	**Dealing with Challenges**	Resilience and persistence; opportunity to grow; face issues head on
Just good enough; no need to stretch myself; not worth it	**Making Efforts**	Desire to achieve and improve; drive to achieve; seeking mastery
Must be avoided; not necessary; get defensive; feedback is for wimps	**Accepting Feedback**	Active and mindful listening; accepting of gaps; willingness to improve; useful
Point fingers; cover yourself; give up easily	**Handling Failure**	Opportunity to learn and try again; springboard to next level

Adapted from Carol Dweck's work

we described in chapter 1. It has some prerequisites. You have to be open to change and experimentation. You have to be more optimistic, or at least recognize the potential for improvement. You have to get yourself into self-development mode. Your aim is to be better than your former self, and better than the competition. If you're unwilling to accept and embrace the value mindset, you will be stuck in old paradigms, old business models, and old ways of doing things. These are not conducive to success.

As mentioned, some people will doubt this process. They'll roll their eyes and try to spread their skepticism. They'll cross their arms and look at you with that look that says "not interested!" But as Dweck says: "Mindsets are fairly stable beliefs, but they are beliefs, and beliefs can be changed."

With a closed or fixed mindset, a value transformation may still be possible but it won't last long. High-quality tools and processes can take a company only so far for so long. We want the changes to stick, and I'll express that even more boldly. We want irreversible change—and that is intimately linked to mindset change. To achieve a successful customer value transformation, you may need to first transform to a value mindset. This book will help inspire you to make that transformation and give you the steps to follow.

One fascinating aspect of a fixed mindset is that it may not be intentional or conscious. As organizational consultants Manfred F. R. Kets de Vries and

Habits
Routines
Frames of reference
Norms
Values
Priorities
Aspirations

mindset (*noun*)

A set of beliefs or a way of thinking that determines one's behavior, outlook, and mental attitude

Irreversible change

Katharina Balazs note, however, this is natural and to be expected.

People have a tendency to hold on to dysfunctional patterns, illogical as these may appear to others. They cannot change their perspective on life without expending a great deal of effort. The reason that many people cling so tenaciously to the status quo is not easy to determine. There are many conscious and unconscious obstacles on the path toward change.

That aspect can make a mindset transformation both necessary and challenging. One problem with a fixed mindset is that during training, it may lead people to interpret instructions as literally as possible. They feel the need to assemble things exactly as described, in that manner and order. They even take comfort in fixed structure and order. Deviations and new ideas can be intimidating. Yet, as I mentioned, we need to break from these robotic approaches and responses. Fortunately, there's a rhyme and reason to that process, and you'll see it unfold as you progress through this book.

The tools and training provided here form the framework and the paradigm. It's up to the individual to develop them further in practice. How one employee might put their training into practice will, and should be, very different from how any other person uses the information. They will have their own good reasons for their interpretation.

Take action with the right people

Changing a fixed mindset to a value mindset helps you overcome or dissolve barriers to change, regardless of whether those barriers are processes, tools, ideas, or even teams. This change happens through training and repetition, retraining, further repetition, and then further training. The pattern repeats until people no longer face change with contempt. In some cases, those who remain unwilling to make any effort to change will be removed or reassigned. But change isn't only about eliminating or neutralizing the negative. You also need an overwhelmingly positive promise. You have to make the mission behind a transformation definite, desirable, aspirational, and attainable, albeit with change and effort. People need to see their own valuable role in the process and in the outcome. There's a lot of truth in Napoleon Hill's statement on the next page.

Packing your tools for this journey of change

Peer-to-peer accountability and organizational accountability can play a big part in helping customers appreciate the value you provide. This internal one-on-one approach links back to the earlier theory of customer value as the glue within the organization. This glue has to be spread by someone with influence on those performing the actions every day and who cares deeply about the people as well as the outcome. Each value transformation will be different because every person and every team is different.

The aggregation of these personal transformations will then lead to an organizational transformation. Bill Taylor discusses the idea of company values and interactions, and of accountability as key, in a *Harvard Business Review* article:

> The most successful leaders and organizations think differently from everyone else. But they also care more than everyone else—about customers, about colleagues, about how the whole organization conducts itself in a world with so many opportunities to cut corners and compromise on values.

Accountability is just one tool for your value transformation journey's ultimate success. Six main components make up the value mindset.

The 6 A's of a Value Mindset

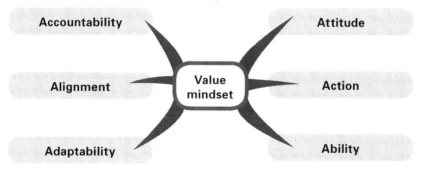

The first three components (right, top to bottom) focus more on the individual within the transformation. Every member of the organization will undergo processes, challenges, and training that they must embrace and continually review. This applies not only to those at the lower levels of the organizational pyramid but also to those in the highest positions of leadership and power. This is also not just about sales. It applies to all key functions involved in the transformation. The efforts and attitudes of everyone involved must be focused in the same direction, from the top of the organization to the very bottom.

The latter set of concepts (left, bottom to top) builds on the individual ones to develop the value transformation as a team. They address what needs to occur in the organization as a whole. The transformation is cumulative. It depends on individual mindsets shifting so that the entire organization acts with a value mindset. This transformation happens person by person, little by little, until the culture of change takes hold of the entire organization and never lets it go! It must then be reinforced with constant value messages and with retraining until an irreversible change occurs. A value mindset is aspirational and powerful for the organization as well as the individual.

During the transformation you'll create internal experts in mindset, value, and change among your staff. These value leaders will possess the skills and training necessary to guide their colleagues, to ensure that they are in the correct mindset to succeed. You'll have a network of value ambassadors who embody this value mindset and who embed themselves in each team. You'll have someone with your value mindset

"There is nothing noble in being superior to your fellow men. True nobility lies in being superior to your former self."

Ernest Hemingway

who reinforces the steps and actions that have an impact. This is how to reach the individuals of the organization and spread the value mindset.

Tracking progress in mindset and value

I strongly recommend that you develop a value dashboard to ensure that employees are using the tools they receive in training. You and your value

leaders will need to focus on maintaining and building morale, and you will also need to have your own value dashboard to track how the transformation and training are going. You'll observe and log questions and answers over time and watch your organization change. The most basic ones are these:

- Are they changing their actions?
- Are they doing their daily actions and practicing a lot?
- Are they being coached on attitude?
- Do we have the right coaching structures in place?
- Do we need to accelerate or reinforce basics again?

Your metrics will evolve, and the process will become more about reinforcement-trained processes and theories than about new actions. The process will accelerate, and the results of the change will be made visible to encourage faster mindset adoption. It's the weightlifting analogy again: immense power comes from achieving ever-increasing stretch goals over an extended period.

Investing in change = Investing in innovation

The true value of the value mindset, a special form of growth mindset, is that it loves the word *can*. As Nicole Lipkin blogged, this transformation to empowerment is the wellspring of innovation.

It is always on the lookout for ways to transcend a problem. Without a growth mindset, we wouldn't have plumbing, or the telephone, or airplanes, or clean water—the list is exhaustive. These all came about because regular people pushed the boundaries and didn't stop when an obstacle presented itself.

The more proactive and intentional you are in fostering and managing the value mindset, the faster your transformation will stick. You make positive change irreversible by preventing employees from falling back into old habits. They will learn to explore and try new things, and new habits will become second nature. The training methods I advocate are different from what you're used to, but they build management and employee skills. Your communication plan will improve, and you will align the attitude and culture in the organization from top to bottom. These are all normal things associated with change management. You don't merely take away the second option that Maslow mentions. A team with a value mindset is always looking forward and no longer even thinks about the safer choice.

So, to make a value mindset stick, you must do the real work after training, and it is ongoing. Consistent feedback will identify and address problems. These feedback rounds may occur daily, weekly, monthly—whichever works best for you—but they must be ongoing. Through these feedback loops, we will reinforce our value mindset—and understand and embrace it—so that we can focus on what we can do as individuals and what we can achieve as an organization.

A value mindset will have positive, everlasting effects. You'll see improved levels of performance, both internally and externally, and happier employees and customers. It's exciting, it's contagious, and it's definitely worth the effort.

Now, let's get started!

Works Cited

Dweck, Carol S. "The Mindset of a Champion." In *Sport and Exercise Psychology: International*

Perspectives, edited by Tony Morris, Peter Terry, and Sandy Gordon (pp. 15–42). Morgantown, WV: Fitness Information Technology, 2007.

Kets de Vries, Manfred F. R., and Katherina Balazs. *Transforming the Mind-Set of the Organization: An Owner's Manual.* Fontainebleau, France: INSEAD, 1996.

Lipkin, Nicole. "The 11 Things You Need for a Growth Mindset." *LinkedIn Pulse,* September 20, 2016, https://www.linkedin .com/pulse/11-things-you-need-growth-mindset-nicole-lipkin-psy-d-m-b-a-.

Taylor, Bill. "Why the Future Belongs to Tough-Minded Optimists." *Harvard Business Review,* March 3, 2016, https://hbr.org/2016/03 /why-the-future-belongs-to-tough-minded -optimists.

Key learning

_____

_____

_____

Key actions

_____

_____

_____

_____

3

A for Attitude

I've WORKED WITH MANY companies and conducted many value transformations. That means I've seen firsthand the power of negativity. Recently, I undertook a value transformation with a very large organization. To begin the process, we did the same thing we're doing in this book: we sat down to talk about mindset.

This was a manufacturing company that also owned a distribution business with $1 billion in annual revenue. The group in the room included the CEO and the VP of marketing, an executive from the distributor, and several other executives and key decision-makers. Despite their diverse roles and backgrounds, they had one thing in common: none of them wanted to hear about problems.

Imagine talking about value transformation with about twenty people behaving in what I would politely describe as a passive-aggressive manner. As you get the ball rolling with some ideas, you notice that some people have shown up only because they're required to attend. Their body language gives them away, and it becomes apparent that they couldn't care less. Surely, if I can see and recognize this attitude, then their colleagues will be dissuaded from speaking up. This is especially true for those who may be a little more introverted or shy but who may have otherwise been willing to make an effort.

And this is precisely what happened.

You could almost see the negativity boiling over, risking that intimidating form of groupthink: total rejection. Such a group refuses to take direction because their mindset is closed. They're not open to the possibility of change. The negative responses range from "no, it isn't going to work" to "we're not going to do it" to "I don't think it's possible to do this in this industry." *These are all excuses, rhetorical deflector shields that direct the discussion away from the real reason behind their collective failure: their unwillingness to change.*

The rationale for change: It's logical, not just emotional

Fortunately, at the other end of the spectrum were a few people who showed a desire to try something new. These individuals had grown tired of seeing results plateau. They wanted improvement. They had a growth mindset. And they bought in to my message for the group:

> What you're doing right now is insanity. You can't keep doing the same thing over and over and expecting different results. You have to look at things differently. You have to try and find other avenues for changing the way you address pricing and value and all of these different avenues. You have to give these new ideas a shot.

While it is easy to deflect blame and make excuses, the underlying logic here is simple and undeniable:

you can't change a bad result without changing the process that created it.

It was amazing to witness this split of attitudes. Despite the passive-aggressiveness and resistance to change in most of the attendees, some fully supported value transformation and the motivation and logic behind it. They understood that maintaining the status quo would never bring different results, and eventually they began giving feedback to the negative people. They challenged them to do something different, to be open to feedback, to be open to the idea, to listen, and to change. The positive attitude came from logic, and it was easier for them to sway the negatives.

Polarized opinions on change are not unique to this company. That is why the first A, attitude, will make or break a value transformation. It's the key attribute. It's at the core of every action you take and will strongly affect your ability to succeed. Every move made at every level of an organization—from the CEO down to the entry-level employee—begins with attitude.

In my experience, attitude is the most decisive factor in whether someone is willing to attempt change

"One must find the source within one's own Self, one must possess it. Everything else was seeking-a detour, an error."

Hermann Hesse

with the goal of improved performance or whether they will resist new ideas and concepts and continue in their old habits. The link between the alignment of values, mindsets, and attitudes is crucial for the success of any transformation.

A blog by Conner Partners summed up for me the critical alignment of value to attitude:

> If the values or goals individuals embrace are not aligned with those needed for successful change, part of the process of reshaping their mindset is to guide them toward priorities that are more consistent with what is needed.

This shaping and reshaping will evolve throughout your journey. It will shape the entire structure of your value transformation.

What are your weaknesses?

A value transformation is a powerful and enduring answer to the question "how can we improve?" with an eye toward better financial and commercial results. The question itself implies that imperfections and weaknesses exist. The first thing to examine during a transformation is the inherent weaknesses you need to neutralize or transform into strengths. This is not easy to address. No one likes talking about their weaknesses, and they may be hard to spot. But it's part of shaping attitude and setting goals.

No one is perfect, but these transformations transcend our own strengths and weaknesses. A value transformation is not about you, your pride, or the past. It's about the team. It's about the future and about new solutions. It's essential to have an open mindset and a positive attitude that lets you open up to new possibilities.

If you enter the transformation with the mindset that everything is working and everything is fine, you're just deflecting the blame toward other parties. Denying the existence of weakness doesn't eliminate it. Instead, it hints at a lack of desire to change, which is often the central problem or weakness. There is always something to improve upon. Therefore, you must have an attitude of openness, a desire to grow and change. If this attitude of positive change begins with management, the odds are even greater that it will quickly permeate the organization.

What self-fulfilling prophecy do you want to fulfill?

There are four prerequisites to the positive attitude manifesting itself:

1 confidence that you can accomplish great things
2 seeing the positives in situations in advance
3 setting measurable and challenging goals
4 anticipating potential roadblocks and previously unforeseen issues.

In "The 11 Things You Need for a Growth Mindset," organizational psychologist Nicole Lipkin touches on the roadblocks to change and on how a company might become more resilient. In her conclusion, she speaks positively of an open attitude being key:

Perhaps most important is a commitment to keeping your mind open to possibility. When obstacles are thrown in our path, the mind has a proclivity to close and react negatively, but it can be trained and harnessed to see possibility rather than doom.

Dr. Lipkin stresses the importance of maintaining this positive attitude—the hope, the resilience, the never-say-die feeling that arises in the face of confrontation. This in turn reinforces confidence. It's a self-fulfilling prophecy. If you have a positive attitude, you will appear confident and in turn become confident. Measuring our own attitudes and actions and setting challenging goals improves our attitudes, enhancing our growth along the journey of self-transformation and value transformation.

Getting rid of cancer

The embodiment of a positive attitude is not the only challenge in value transformation. You must eliminate and eradicate negative attitudes as well. This requires concerted effort. Negativity can spread like a cancer in an organization, especially in working teams and training sessions.

Polarized attitudes are not isolated events. That's why I began this chapter with the story of the management meeting. I've seen this polarization in most, if not all, of the value transformations I've facilitated. If you use your emotional intelligence to recognize this polarization, you can gain an edge in your transformation. By identifying the pockets of positive attitude in the room, you can encourage those pockets to help eradicate the cancer of negativity. Even when you're talking to executives and CEOs of large companies who are denying or rejecting any basis for change, there is still hope for change.

Entry-level employees and junior managers can also become powerful agents for change, if you can encourage them to share their views. If you're serious about change, it's critical to impart that your place in the organization isn't as important as your attitude. If you show an attitude of enthusiasm and a willingness to lead, you can influence others to adopt a positive outlook.

I can't stress this point enough: if you're attempting to make a transformation and you have bad apples in the room, regardless of position or status, they can be a cancer on the team.

Sometimes these negative attitudes are cultural and not personal. A multicultural team can erode from the inside out if some team members come from a culture that's more pessimistic or more reserved.

When individuals are less friendly, or are less willing to open up and experiment, the entire group suffers. It kills the spirit. It kills the hope that we can get this done as a team, and it's challenging for those who are trying to enact change as well as for those who are willing to learn. It's up to the team members to use their positive attitude actively—not to send this cancer into remission but to eliminate it.

Are you training for change?

Meetings with CEOs and senior management are not the only place you might encounter a poor attitude, manifested in a reluctance to accept change. I've observed it frequently in company-wide training programs.

There are always people in the room who have a fixed mindset. They see the training as a waste of time. Generally, you will always encounter some pushback from fixed-mindset individuals as you try to move them beyond their comfort zones to instigate change. To succeed, you will need to address the bad attitude or the fixed mindset. Attitude is not only a vital prerequisite for a value transformation. It's also the first one that needs to change. The attitudes "no, it's not going to happen," "no, it's never going to work," and "I don't want to make the effort" will slow the launch of the transformation. Without a positive attitude from the entire team, you'll be mired in good intentions, not moving forward.

These negative attitudes toward training come from a variety of sources. They might reflect previous experiences with poor training exercises or come from negative hearsay from colleagues. There's often a grain of truth in these assessments. Sometimes a company's poor approach to training is the root cause of a bad attitude. Poor training after poor training without success translates to poor, fixed mindsets among employees and then reinforces those mindsets. Who is willing to experiment when their expectations for training—based on real experience—have sunk so low?

To fix the attitude and change the mindset, you need to change the training, perhaps everything from the frequency to the approach to the content. If trainers fail to change their actions or refocus their efforts, they unwittingly contribute to the same stagnation that the value transformation is intended to prevent or eliminate.

My approach to fixing this aims at separating the new training from past experiences and past training to prevent these negative attitudes from taking hold or being further reinforced. You need a clean break, a fresh start; and you need to communicate it openly as such. Once I have people's attention, especially the attention of those with a fixed mindset, I try to tackle new issues and to inform and provide new processes and concepts. I try to do this in ways that give the trainees enjoyable tasks in the training, but I remain adaptable and pay attention to how the trainees respond. Companies should invest more carefully and more wisely in different training programs. A transformative training program alone can change attitudes and foster a more open mindset.

The power of contagion: Cultivating positivity

In all my experiences around the world with value transformations, one fact has stood out: attitude, whether positive or negative, is contagious. This motivates me when I design and implement new training models. A positive attitude can spread like wildfire throughout a team and a whole organization. It can have a unifying effect. It can elevate the organization to the great success we've all hoped for. But a negative attitude can spread the same way if you give it the fuel it needs. These rapidly spreading negative attitudes lead to division and devastation.

This contagious nature of attitude is what we need to harness.

To enter a transformational mode—a truly inspirational and motivating experience where you enter the hearts and the minds of many people—you need the best people with the best attitudes. You need the people who are charismatic, who share your vision, and who are communicating their positive energy and attitude to their colleagues. Then you use the contagious nature of attitude to accelerate the transformation process. You let these people lead the training or the coaching programs, allowing them as many touch points and opportunities as possible to impart what they've learned and embraced. As a bonus, their peers and colleagues will be more willing to learn and to accept advice and feedback from them in a positive manner than they would from an outside trainer or speaker.

This sends a strong and clear message to human resources: hire for attitude.

When you do a value transformation, you will inevitably lose people. It's fantasy to think that you'll convert every one of your existing team members; and at some point, you'll see diminishing returns. Some people will resign and others will be transferred as roles and responsibilities become more fluid as changes take hold. In the worst case, you may need to let people go. To keep the business going, not just the transformation, you need to restock talent as people move on.

Attitude must become the number-one criterion for selecting new people.

Remember: you're not just looking for new employees—you're looking for new leaders. Whether new marketing people or salespeople or receptionists, you want whoever is involved in this project to have a positive outlook, a willingness to self-evolve, and a willingness to experiment. Everyone in the company during and following a transformation needs to embrace feedback and to get up when they fail. It will become imperative from this point forward to hire for attitude, not just for skill.

"The optimist lives on the peninsula of infinite possibilities; the pessimist is stranded on the island of perpetual indecision."

William Arthur Ward

So as a golden rule, when you recruit for people on these project teams, in training programs, or in the organization, hire for attitude and not just for skill. These are the individuals who can lead. They are the ones you can depend on to further elevate and enhance the attitude throughout your entire organization.

Attitude shapes the future

In a *Harvard Business Review* article, Bill Taylor, a co-founder of the magazine *Fast Company,* stated:

The future is not shaped by people who don't really believe in the future, it is created by highly motivated people, by enthusiasts, by men and women who want something very much or believe very much.

The best leaders have all sorts of skills and use all kinds of techniques, but there is no substitute "for the lift of spirit and heightened performance that comes from strong motivation." It is exactly these motivated and optimistic people that you want to hire in your business.

It all begins with the right attitude.

Key learning

_____

_____

_____

_____

Key actions

_____

_____

_____

_____

4

A for Action

© LIOZU 2017

W E'VE ALL EXPERIENCED A trainer who ends a session by saying "tomorrow, you will take actions A, B, and C." At the time, the assignment may make perfect sense. Then we leave the room, return to our jobs, and the connections become less clear.

What was I supposed to do? How was I supposed to do it?

In the immediate aftermath of a training phase, there is usually an element of confusion. Even when employees fully understood the training, applying the training can prove more difficult. You can tell employees whatever you want. But without further elaboration, you're simply assuming that people will act on your orders and advice. You assume they'll process the training in a way that they can apply to their jobs. You assume that they can self-organize to prioritize and perform the actions you've given them.

That's a lot of assumptions!

Unfortunately, action is not that simple. And asking for a repetition of actions is even more daring. You can't talk your way to success. Orders and requests after training don't automatically lead to action. This has many root causes. First, each of us processes and interprets instructions differently. Second, some people are not action-oriented. Third, some people are unwilling to try anything outside of their comfort zone. They have a fixed mindset.

In such cases, I tell the teams that we will have a coaching session. We will learn how to turn training into action. People take action when we give them the tools and frameworks to continue on their journey and further their own self-transformation. Action allows us to move beyond the theoretical part of our journey. We take what we've learned in training and implement it with the expectation of specific results.

To allow action, you must empower

The first step in moving from training to the real world is to assign more leadership roles. Your employees have been taking part in different activities and exercises during training. They've learned to adapt to multicultural and multifunctional roles and to identify their own transformation process. Of course, developing leaders requires providing feedback and further development, a support track on which the employees can continue their journey.

Coaching will not only empower your employees but also identify new leaders. A key identifying marker for these leaders is the existence of a value mindset, which should become apparent through feedback talks and through their own plans and thoughts for further development. Through coaching and feedback sessions, you can seek out those who show an accelerated growth mindset, those who may be moving faster in their journey and can directly or indirectly inspire others to act as well. You empower them to pass along their contagious attitude. I call these people value champions. They are embedded "agents" who accelerate transformation in the field, at headquarters, or in remote locations. Because they get it, they become your ally to support and energize daily actions by those who might be in the late majority for change.

One secret to action: Write it down

Your primary tool in this part of the journey is simple, yet critical to your success: a value log, or value journal. I propose an example of value journal in the Resources section. I've seen its benefits firsthand and believe it can reaffirm not only your transformation as an organization but also the transformation of each employee. Individuals track their steps, their actions, their thoughts, and their affirmations in this log. Writing it down—itself a simple but powerful action—will give them a tangible reminder of their commitment and of the theory and processes they learned in training.

One could argue that having your team write down *something* every day, no matter what or how much, is valuable on its own. While I agree in principle, and prefer to have individuals find their own best way to keep a value log, I've learned over time which approaches work better than others. My method in coaching is to ask individuals to enter two or three very specific things they are going to do the next week in the log. With these tasks recorded, either a leader or I will follow up on each item. I call this dynamic feedback. You cannot wait too long to give feedback, especially when it comes to potentially disruptive practices. Feedback needs to be specific and timely. Not everyone will appreciate this scrutiny, at least at first. Over time, however, they'll recognize the helpfulness of accountability, both to themselves and to their leaders. As they continue to use their value logs, they will ultimately discover improved performance in all aspects of their work. This approach is similar to goal setting on a personal level, but with additional motivation and accountability. I've seen it used repeatedly to brilliant effect.

Do or do not: Trying is no longer an option

Try sounds like such a positive word. It implies willingness, effort, optimism, and a healthy attitude, right? So what would you think if I told you that *try* is a yellow flag or even a red flag in your feedback discussions? It's true.

Do is the verb of people with a value mindset. *Try* is an imposter for a value mindset.

Employees who use the word *try* in performance reviews tend to be the ones who are not quite getting the work done and not quite hitting their targets. Their projects are chronically behind. They embody why a value transformation is difficult and necessary and why it requires a commitment of time and support as well as the right mindset.

Trying allows for a lot of ambiguity and built-in excuses, should a task or effort lead to failure. A famous movie quote from the *Star Wars* anthology

"Try not.
Do, or do not.
There is no try."

Jedi Master Yoda

springs to mind. Jedi master Yoda reminds the young Luke Skywalker of the message above.

On certain occasions, you may encounter employees saying "Well, I tried to do this" or "I tried it that way and it didn't work." These instances are where we need to supply positive affirmation. Our leaders must instill the notion that there is no try, that the worker believes "I am going to do it" and then will later move on to other, more ambitious tasks that will increase and reinforce their sense of accomplishment. The mindset moves from *try* to *do,* and translates into action. It becomes embedded in a precise, concrete, and measurable process.

Motivating action

Action, particularly the reinforcing action of the value log, is a critical component of transformation success. But if we want these actions to become patterns, we

need to inspire our employees—and everyone—to follow these processes.

Transformation is designed not only for the usual
suspects of the account managers and salespeople but
also for top executives. Those at the top of the hierarchy might also be at the top of the transformational
pyramid, inspiring others to follow their behaviors.
Doing a value transformation from the bottom up
may turn into a great story to tell, but a transformation with strong top-down influence will usually move
faster and more efficiently. Therefore, those at the top
of the pyramid must be just as willing to track their
actions and log their progress as those in the middle
or at the base. Action relies on people actually doing
things to generate momentum in the transformation.
Every organizational level must make time and space
for it in their schedules and be committed to inspire
other levels. This is how actions transcend the existing hierarchy.

But motivating action is more than just having the
leaders demonstrate that they're doing the same thing
as the subordinates. Setting realistic goals, and eas-
ing in the new transformation, will also help ingrain
these actions as daily activities. You want to get the
employees started on the post-training transformation as soon as you can, but it is just as important not
to be overzealous. Success is a motivator; you want to
give people things to do, but you must not give them
extremely difficult tasks with unrealistic time limits.
Overloading them with tasks and actions they cannot

possibly complete will undermine their self-worth and take you backward from the hardwired results of *do* to the soft excuses of *try*. This can endanger the entire journey's success.

Start with easier tasks:

- Ask them to write a self-reflection daily or weekly.
- Instruct them to convey a value message to a client.
- Ask them to complete some personal homework on the client, for instance something as simple as finding out who is a value buyer versus a price buyer.
- Communicate a value message, designed and rehearsed in our training, to a customer.

This is where your team sees the difference between developing the value message and believing it. The latter demands daily implementation but doesn't need to be difficult or daunting. One step in the training is to ask participants to design value messaging we can use the next day and many days thereafter. Employees can build a framework around these messages and hone their customer-facing skills. I ask participants to introduce the value message into their work the next day.

One such value message might come from the "Did you know?" technique.

"Did you know we invented that product? Did you know we've sold a billion units? Did you know that . . . ?" Like the value journal, this technique is incredibly simple. All it requires is discovering one or two facts about the organization that are transferable across all platforms and then mentioning them in conversation with the customer. It's a simple value message that translates to a simple and practical goal. You've given people a concrete, doable action to employ and log in their journal immediately, instilling pride in a small but important job already complete.

An idea drives the transformation process from the theoretical and cerebral to the concrete when you turn that idea into something very practical. I found a good summary of this point in a *Harvard Business Review* article, by John Butman:

An idea is an abstraction that won't produce change until you provide people with specific, practical ways to put it into everyday use.

But the team must also take the action seriously, regardless of whether the task is internal or external, client- or individual-based. The person charged with the task must report to someone who has a leadership role. That leader must examine the results, provide feedback, validate the *done* and push back against the *tried*. Repetition of this process will lead to improved results and to overall success of the transformation. Smaller, simpler, practical tasks will provide more opportunities to reinforce the process. Ultimately, we all want these transformations to be self-sustaining, with less and less supervision required. Employees may resist the scrutiny, but as anyone who has taken part in a value transformation knows all too well, trust is earned, and accountability is a skill to cultivate, not a presumption to make.

Raising the bar: Upping the actions and increasing efficiency

Let's say you've had the value logs in place for some time. Your team is used to logging and tracking tasks consistently. The best next step, in my experience, is to step back.

The goal is not to stop or stall the progress. The goal is to accelerate it.

You should reassess how the team is doing. If most have adjusted to the actions, and the attitude is increasingly positive, then it's time to start raising both the difficulty and the intensity of the actions. As more time passes, and employees get better at their initial tasks (e.g., better at value messaging), it's then possible to extend these techniques and processes to other actions and abilities.

At the end of this first stage, leading up to the reassessment, you will have experts in their fields, confident in the value they add and well versed in the value their company adds. You are on your way to transforming your team into value action experts. This will save time on overall value transformation. Now you have an entire team who can perform value score-carding and value logging, and who are ready for the more complex steps in the value transformation that we will discuss.

Action will take some back-and-forth, from training to practice to training again. Though it feels slower at first to take an occasional step back on purpose, this pause helps perfect the method and instills the right behaviors. A key point here is to trust the training and its ability to build skills and instill a value mindset within your workforce. If you learn how much you've changed, and how and why you've changed so much, you can design the next training, which will initiate another process. This is how the process of continued improvement succeeds.

The back-and-forth between training and practice almost mirrors the overlapping nature of the first two As—attitude and action—and this combination of processes and paradigms is critical in creating change. After all, that is the initial goal of this journey. When we do a mindset transformation, we are not only making irreversible change, but also change that over the long run will make business smoother and more successful. Attitude, action, training, and practice are some of the key interrelated components.

It's a tough journey: Keeping your head during the transformation

It's foolish to think that a value transformation is easy or that any part of it is automatic. It's more like a manual transmission in a car, where you can only shift gears and accelerate when you are hands-on and take a specific coordinated action. There's no

"Courage is never to let your actions be influenced by your fears."

Arthur Koestler

gas pedal allowing you to accelerate by comfortably applying more pressure.

Success in value transformation requires a growth mindset and a different perspective on what learning and training mean in the business world. You may have to unlearn everything you've been taught about commercial and organizational training. You will need to accept that, from here on out, you're going to do most things differently.

Slow acceptance of that idea can sometimes cause a transformation to break down. As a trainer and a coach, I see a lot of frustration on all sides when the people brought in to help are unwilling to participate and learn. Again, I'm not talking only about the individuals at the bottom of the organizational pyramid. The biggest obstacles can be at the top, in some cases the very people who brought me in to help enact the transformation.

Traditional training is dead. Long live training!

In chapter 3 we discussed how attitudes must change to begin the process. Actions must also reflect an acceptance of change to keep the process from derailing. You need to allocate adequate time and resources to the training and make allowances to put the training into action. This can require you to change your perception of what training is all about in the organization and what your employees think the training is all about.

For instance, I don't usually refer to it as training. I like to think of it as rewiring. You put employees into a mode of self-development instead of the mode they are used to in training, which is more about listening than doing. Many people expect to sit and listen to lectures, not focused at all on what they should be taking away from it. But the obligation for change is not only on the participants. Yes, there is such a thing as bad training. It may be boring, or have insufficient or outdated content, or give people unrealistic expectations. No matter the cause, the bottom line is that training is only effective when it leads to the desired actions. Anything else is the instructional equivalent of *try.*

For training to lead to a *do* mentality, organizations need to embrace new teaching and learning styles. Learning is constant. It's in everything we do and in every decision. Proper, action-oriented training can teach us to learn better. Training must become a constant and never-ending process and a way of life, instead of a disposable good, a few hours each month to listen and then forget.

The more you do something successfully, the more you will want to do it, and the more confidence you'll have in yourself. In business this will create a snowball effect, building confidence not only in the individual but as a team. As we've discussed, initial actions do not have to be particularly difficult or strenuous. They can be simple. The important part is practice and repetition until the action becomes your second nature. Then and only then can you move on to more difficult ones. Small actions repeated often lead to incremental improvements, which will become irreversible. Repeated over time, this will create a new frame of reference and new routines throughout the hierarchy.

You cannot expect to make one big change, put it into action once, and expect its effects to endure. The mantra has to be *small actions, many actions, every day.* Think of a professional golfer learning to change a particular swing. If they make one big change but

"I fear not the man who practiced 10,000 kicks once, I fear the man who practiced one kick 10,000 times."

Bruce Lee

don't practice it over and over again, it will never stick. They will soon revert to the old swing, and any improvements and adjustments will be lost in the wasted time and effort. If instead they focus on making a small change, they can practice it relentlessly until the change becomes routine. Then they can make further changes in the same simple manner. Each adjustment then becomes irreversible change, which elevates the golfer to greater success.

Now substitute "professional golfer" with "salesperson," and "changing a swing" with "imparting better value messages to customers." We now have a simple explanation of actions needed within a value transformation: simple, easily repeated, and each building on the last goal. Couple this with the idea of a value log or journal, and we have a recipe for continued success.

If you don't want to take my word for it, I highly recommend the article "How 1% Performance Improvements Led to Olympic Gold," from *Harvard Business Review*. It explains how the British cycling team won seven gold medals at the 2008 Olympics after winning only one medal in the previous 76 years. Their secrets: strategy, a growth mindset, and an emphasis on continuous incremental improvement.

Taking the next step: Mapping your journey

Essential to the *action* part of the transformation are the four key values I've listed in the value mindset assessment in the Resources section. You can use these when monitoring your own individual progress or that of your employees. Put simply, we need to do these four things to make sure our actions become second nature and lead to positive and irreversible results. Refer to them often as you continue your journey.

- Have a clear list of daily actions to take that support value programs.
- Concretely apply what you learn in training, and transform learning into practical activities.
- Have value tools, such as logs, that reinforce the need to practice our value programs each day.
- Receive and give feedback and coaching on personal action plans to improve performance with value programs continually.

Works Cited

Butman, John. "Idea Entrepreneur: The New 21st
Century Career." *Harvard Business Review,*
May 23, 2013, https://hbr.org/2013/05/
idea-entrepreneur-the-new-21st.
Harrell, Eben. "How 1% Performance Improvements Led to Olympic Gold." *Harvard Business Review,* October 30, 2015, https://hbr.
org/2015/10/how-1-performance-improvements-
led-to-olympic-gold.

Key learning

_____

_____

_____

_____

Key actions

_____

_____

_____

_____

5

A for Ability

© LIOZU 2017

THE BUSINESS WORLD, AND indeed the world as a whole, overemphasizes failure. We are surrounded by constant scrutiny that can blow even the smallest mistakes out of proportion. Everything from big errors to minor missteps can show up on the screens of phones and tablets around the world, even those of people we've never met. While this social media availability is barely two decades old (remarkable, right?), it has amplified something inherent in human nature: we are risk averse, and afraid to take chances, not only because we might fail but because failure brings even more unexpected and negative consequences.

I bring up failure in a chapter about ability for two reasons. First, in business, what we call a failure is rarely fatal or final. This isn't just an inspirational cliché out of Silicon Valley, where failure is considered a rite of passage. What we call failure can serve as a powerful diagnostic tool to indicate the presence of ability or mask true ability. Failure can also be the precursor to success, once we take a close and more objective look at it. In its simplest form, failure at a given task occurs through a weakness in ability, process, or effort. You might be tempted to add target or goal to that list, because it's easy to get discouraged when we think of a goal as difficult to achieve, if not impossible. But history has shown repeatedly that we don't know what we are capable of—or the great places our work and effort will lead us—until we try.

Take the anecdote that gained worldwide attention in the movie *The Martian*. Back in the 1930s, a group of friends were kicked out of their dormitory at CalTech for what seems like an obvious reason: they blew up their dorm room. Was that mistake final and fatal for them? Far from it! A professor at CalTech was keen enough to recognize two things in the young men: ability and effort. He helped them gain space and materials to continue their explosive experiments. At that time they could have hardly imagined that their pioneering work would lead to the creation of the Jet Propulsion Laboratory, which prepares and manages space missions for NASA.

This leads to my second reason for mentioning failure in the chapter on ability. When we think of both success and failure as functions of ability, process, and effort, we are in a much better position to help teams succeed at complex undertakings such as a value transformation. We appreciate that we can recognize, measure, and improve ability and process. And we can cultivate an attitude that fosters the willingness to overcome risk aversion and explore and mine "failure" for its lessons and benefits. Remember, we are on a journey, and journeys have detours, setbacks, and wrong turns. Yet it's precisely on such long journeys that we discover how capable we are, what abilities we have, and how we can get the most out of them.

Honing your team's ability and its willingness to accept change is a crucial component of getting

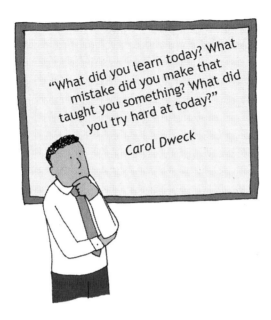

"What did you learn today? What mistake did you make that taught you something? What did you try hard at today?"

Carol Dweck

improved results. This is what makes a value transformation stick. Recent research published in the *Harvard Business Review* suggests that

> managers who completed a training program designed to build greater belief in the potential for employee development were subsequently more willing to coach a poorly performing employee, and also provided more and higher quality suggestions for improvement.

It makes sense to design training to address specific gaps in ability. But this finding also reveals a bigger message, which brings us back to the idea of a fixed mindset versus a growth mindset. Based on my experience, and on the research of many others who have studied success, failure, and training, I draw one inescapable conclusion: ability is **not** a fixed quantity.

In a literal sense, ability refers to the innate capacity and competence of an individual to complete a given task. It's synonymous with talent, proficiency, and skill. Ability is similar to mindset in that it's often viewed as fixed, or limited. In reality, ability is expandable and transferable to a large degree. It's something we can grow and nurture, in ourselves and in others.

Building on that statement, we can also conclude that in the process of a value transformation each individual becomes more proficient and more skilled. A value transformation is not only about financial and commercial results. It's up to management, with the help of the training staff, to create the right conditions and structures to identify, nurture, and capitalize on

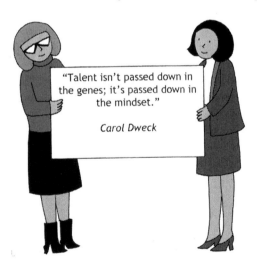

"Talent isn't passed down in the genes; it's passed down in the mindset."

Carol Dweck

the abilities of each individual. In other words, management must understand the abilities and potential of each individual, and then put the team in a position to succeed against the goals it has set. At the same time, it's also up to the individual to engage and commit to some self-exploration, for example with the value logs.

Imagine the power a group of individuals can unleash when it improves ability, process, and effort simultaneously!

Setting the stage for value growth

The rest of this chapter focuses on creating the right conditions and structures to identify and improve ability. These conditions and structures set the stage for value growth. That means an emphasis on training. Once again, we take guidance from Carol Dweck, who noted this in her section on sports psychology:

> View talents as potentialities that can be developed through practice. It's not that people holding this mindset deny differences among people. They don't deny that some people may be better or faster than others at acquiring certain skills, but what they focus on is the idea that everyone can get better over time.

Despite this attitude, some team members will roll their eyes when they hear that additional training will take place. We need to be careful when we encounter such skepticism. It doesn't necessarily mean that the team feels they're already fully capable, or that they see their abilities as fixed or maxed out. It often means that they don't want more boring training or training for training's sake. Unfortunately, research has demonstrated that many prevailing corporate training methods are outdated, even obsolete. In our context, it means that they don't provide adequate conditions and structures for growth.

We will need to redefine and implement new ways to help individuals and teams enhance and enrich their ability. Successful value transformations in other organizations can guide us.

For starters, *how* we train is often more decisive than *what* we train. It comes back to mindset. We have to excite not only our employees but also ourselves about training. We have to add something new, something exciting that makes learning desirable and easier for individuals to absorb and apply the content and thus enhance their abilities. If success at a given task is part ability, part process, and part effort, then we need to make sure that training builds and inspires in all of those areas.

The improvement equation is ability plus the willingness to improve (mindset), the opportunity to improve (training, tasks, practice), and the effort to improve (commitment). Viewed from this perspective, it's easy to see that empowerment through training may require a format change. Neither lecturing over long sessions nor bombarding employees with

"No matter what your ability is, effort is what ignites that ability and turns it into accomplishment."

Carol Dweck

multiple concepts over very short sessions is effective. If you want to train for growth, it's vital to introduce dynamic, differentiated, and diversified training that reaches employees at an emotional level and not merely at an intellectual one.

This means much of the training must also focus on effort, attitude, and personal actions. These manifest themselves in habits, and habits are always difficult to change. I take a different perspective on this and challenge the team to think about whether habits are masking their true abilities. Habits keep them from improving. If they only knew how good can they be!

Remember: You're training for growth

When working through the ability aspect of the value transformation, we need to be innovative in how we define and enable the ability-building process. We must change the vocabulary and the learning culture. We need to focus not only on results but also on the process and the effort to generate those results. It's important to remember that an organization as a whole doesn't unilaterally decide to adopt change. Living, breathing people need to make decisions and act on them, because any organization is really a collection of individuals who aim higher because they know they are capable of more.

Role-play can serve as an integral part of the training process, especially when teams have a chance to assume unfamiliar roles, or roles that turn the tables. Let marketing and sales switch roles. Let the financial team and product development get a taste of what the others do. Observing how the teams perform in these roles can develop empathy, helping each team see that all others are pulling in the same direction in a value transformation, just in their own way. It can also foster greater recognition and validation of existing abilities, setting the stage for improvement and growth.

Does ability have natural limits?

Training for growth also means asking "where do we go from here?" Improving one's ability may have theoretical natural limits, but I doubt that most people in any organization know where those limits are. Do you know with any precision how good you can be? I dare you to say that you've maxed out in any of your abilities, at least those abilities that contribute to your well-being and urge you to keep improving. And what happens if you rest on your laurels or minimize effort because you think you can get by on your innate talents? Dweck calls out this risk of complacency, both as a warning and as an inspiration to work hard:

Sure "natural talent" buys you a lot, and if you're accomplished now, you've got a leg up on others. But after that you cannot know where someone might end up with years of passion, discipline, and commitment—and good instruction.

Beware of value robots

Differentiation and diversity in training also matter if you want to train for growth and improve abilities. The objective of a value transformation is not to turn your people into value robots who say and do exactly as they're told. That robotic mentality is the hallmark of the front-of-the-classroom lecture format, where the same people sit through the same things regardless of the natural talent they possess, the effort they put in, or the progress they've made. I encourage you to experiment when applying the tools in this book. I also encourage you to define abilities in different ways. We often think of abilities in the sense of a narrow job description, such as proficiency with a software package, knowledge of accounting or engineering, or a trade skill. This approach risks neglecting soft skills, interpersonal skills, and other underestimated abilities such as critical thinking. I would even say that teaching and learning are essential skills. Define the set of abilities your team possesses—and the needs you should address—more broadly than what you see in today's job descriptions from human resources.

That encouragement also comes through in this statement from change coach and management academic Monique Valcour, in a recent *Harvard Business Review* article:

When you face a learning challenge, brainstorm different strategies you can use to stretch yourself, experiment with them, and keep track of what works best. This will help you focus on the learning process and develop flexible learning strategies.

This statement encompasses everything I've been saying. On a managerial level at the top of the organizational pyramid, you must embrace and encourage the transformation process. You need to put your teams in a position to succeed by setting a goal; directing ability, process, and effort toward that goal; and actively working to improve all three. At the same time, individuals must be prepared to take the tools, learn them, and adapt them based on their situation, environment, and the way they interact with their customers and peers.

Why effort makes a difference

Change means opportunity, and when opportunities appear, we need to embrace them. This is easy to say but harder to do. Companies often take evasive action when change comes. This is risk aversion not because of an objective weighing of the consequences but often because of an unwillingness to make the effort. Witness this common business situation, which you yourself many have encountered.

An issue arises requiring a price change. The company puts people in a room and gives them the same boring training and speeches as always. The people hear "We're going to make it through this issue; we're going to be successful. We're going to raise prices!"

Then no major change occurs. We avoid change and taking action because we fear failing worse than we fear the issue.

Invariably, the same issue, the same opportunity, reappears. Trying the same thing repeatedly and expecting different results is the definition of insanity. And in business it doesn't work. This is not about a lack of ability, and in many cases not even a lack of process. It's about a lack of effort. Isn't it time to do something different?

The antidote to this business insanity is effort.

Effective transformation: Checking your conditions and structures

Let's now look back to the value mindset assessment provided throughout this book and see where the responsibility lies for creating the conditions and the structures for a team to succeed to the best of its (expandable!) abilities. Check to make sure you satisfy each requirement:

1 **Have we received proper training in all relevant dimensions of value management?** Ensure that you've chosen the best possible transformation guides and training experts to engage your employees, not merely instruct them. The impetus for this must come from the top of the organization. Leadership needs to recognize that the same equation (ability + process + effort) defines both success and

failure. Failure is nothing more than a sign that we need to fix one or more of the variables; it's not a sign of shame or a sign that the game is over. Get to work!

2 **Have we been able to practice and experiment with new tools, methods, and concepts before introducing them to the market?** It's imperative that everyone have time to adapt to and practice their new or improved skills. Management has an obligation to provide time and space for this, as I elaborate in the next chapter.

3 **Have we absorbed the knowledge from the best practices, value success stories, external benchmarks, and lessons learned?** Training doesn't end when the "training" ends. We're always learning and always reinforcing what we've learned. Here the responsibility lies with all parties involved. Management must do its utmost to nurture and reinforce the messages and best practices conveyed through the training. Individuals need to put in the effort to live out the messages and lessons rom the training as well.

4 **Do we have access to value experts, coaches, and supplemental training when we need reinforcement on key value concepts?** It's not enough to do something once or train for a couple of hours while sitting in a room and then expect immediate wholesale changes throughout the organization. This requires reinforcement and ongoing guidance. It takes time. Place value leaders and coaches on

your teams so they can give and receive feedback. Additional, regular training will help cement the irreversible change we seek.

The previous three chapters primarily addressed individual concerns and the use of a one-on-one approach. Over the next three chapters—covering the rest of the As—we look a little more deeply at team-wide approaches.

But before we move on, here's a final note about what can happen if we use failure as a proxy for ability and assign too much weight to previous mistakes.

Imagine you're selecting teams for a basketball game at the playground. You're considering choosing the tall guy on the end, when someone whispers in your ear *Him? You can't be serious! He's lost 300 games! He's missed, like, over 9,000 shots. And when his teams have had a chance to win, they let him take the last shot and he's missed over 25 times.*

Nervous, you pick someone else.

After the game—which you lost horribly—you walk over, somewhat embarrassed, to the tall guy you didn't pick. You extend your hand and introduce yourself.

His name? Michael Jordan.

Works Cited

Dweck, Carol S. "The Mindset of a Champion." In *Sport and Exercise Psychology: International Perspectives,* edited by T. Morris, P. Terry, and

S. Gordon (pp. 15–42). Morgantown, WV: Fitness Information Technology, 2007.

Valcour, Monique. "People Won't Grow If You Think They Can't Change." *Harvard Business Review,* April 21, 2016, https://hbr.org/2016/04/people-wont-grow-if-you-think-they-cant-change.

Key learning

_____

_____

_____

_____

Key actions

_____

_____

_____

_____

A for Adaptability

6

THE VALUE CHAMPION

THERE'S A STORY ABOUT NASA which may be urban legend but still makes a relevant point for value transformations. Supposedly the first Apollo mission to reach the moon was off course over 90 percent of the time. Course corrections, both major and minor, helped the manned rocket reach its destination and then return safely.

This anecdote offers an important insight for a company that has embarked on a value transformation. The ultimate long-term goal may remain clear and unwavering, but the path to that goal is anything but a straight line. Zigging and zagging, even occasionally pausing or backtracking, are the reality of this journey. Such moments should not be surprises.

Value transformation evolves much more smoothly when everyone recognizes that change is a flow and not a moment. Achieving the overall (directional) change is the sum of all the small changes and adjustments we make along the way. Ability, as we discussed in chapter 5, is essential and is something each individual can and should improve. But ability is not sufficient for long-term survival without adaptability

Of course, any change will be met with some initial internal opposition. No matter when or how you enact your transformation, you will run into artificial obstacles and common excuses:

"We don't have time."

"Now is not the right time."

"The market is crashing. We have more urgent things to do."

"That's not the way we do things around here."

And these are only what you hear people vocalize. A good leader and change manager must sense the unspoken questions and sentiment when the team leaves the room after a meeting. You need to anticipate them and address them. The empathy you demonstrate through this awareness and recognition will help you build allies as you eliminate some uncertainty and doubt.

These spoken and unspoken excuses arise time after time when an organization attempts a value transformation. They can crop up from the individual employee all the way up through management and executive levels. When the first course deviation comes, these naysayers will seize the opportunity to say "I told you so" and rally more people to their resistance.

Because you know this will happen—trust me, it will—you need to get out in front of it. Positive advance communication is essential to keeping people motivated and managing their expectations. You can't afford to wait for the unwilling to accept change and come around. This is what it means to drive change actively and vigorously within an organization. Don't let failures or setbacks feed the opposition. Help them define the next step and the course correction.

As they say in the military, the first casualty of any battle is the plan. You need to adapt, redraw the map, and learn as you go, because the ultimate goal remains the same. A transformation is an ongoing

journey with many routes and processes. It takes a lot of time and effort. This means you have to adapt. Perhaps Charles Darwin said it best.

Adaptability and multitasking

Adaptability during a value transformation means being able to switch smoothly between old and new processes until they blend into a unified and aligned way of doing business. Call it juggling, call it multitasking, call it the ambidextrous organization. Any way you frame it, teams that become adept at switching hands on the fly improve their chances of success.

Running the bulk of your day-to-day operations in the existing way while also incorporating new, more promising measures makes this an extremely complex situation. You cannot make a wholesale change concentrated at one point in time. That would be impossible. The theory of evolution may apply to business ("survival of the fittest") but the big bang theory does not. You have to simultaneously manage existing methods and operations, learn how to do things better, and shape your future by managing new processes and actions.

Trying to get your current employees to carry out their regular jobs and cultivate the transformation is untenable without proper support, encouragement, and rewards. Doing so would mean the very people you are dumping this new workload on are already working ten hours a day or fifty hours a week. Usually there is already a lot of complexity within the company. You cannot expect employees to be happy or productive under this increased workload unless you take actions to help them drive change. As much as I stress communication, words are not enough. Your people are already working on lots of projects, including many so-called strategic initiatives. Now you're asking them to perform a value transformation too?

Set a small but strong list of priorities

The challenge is to figure out how best to lead people into thinking differently and adapting when they already have too many priorities. Some of these changes may be far-reaching and fundamental, such as a new business model, a new pricing approach, an intense focus on a smaller number of customer segments, or the beginning of a transition from a product-driven company to a service-driven one. You must manage two things at once, but this juggling will not last forever.

This is where challenges really add up and adaptability becomes paramount. The company is busy, teams are busy, and individual people are busy. They have things to sell, quotas to hit, profit margins to expand, and deadlines to meet. At the same time, you're asking them to do something new and make a major transition. The only way you can transition from the old to the new is by creating an atmosphere of freedom and encouragement so that individuals feel at liberty to play around and experiment. This, in essence, is what generates adaptability within individuals.

Companies meet this challenge well when they reduce some of their existing processes at the lower level. Of course, this approach can become a major problem with some current executives. They don't want to see decreased activity and may not want to accept that some short-term pain is necessary for long-term gain. Instead, they believe they can keep adding to people's plates and expect everything to be done properly and efficiently. These leaders need to adapt their mindset as well and invest in the change.

They need to realize when they are smothering their employees and stifling progress.

In the end, you're defeating your own transformation when you only add to priority lists rather than help teams understand the right balance between important and urgent and accomplish what they can.

This is when the adaptability of the organization—its willingness to change, to deal with the unexpected, and to remain focused on the ultimate goal—plays its most important role. But you have to drive change and encourage and reward this adaptability. It never happens on its own, and it's hard enough when you actively pursue it.

Accelerating the adaptation, but at the team's pace

When we talk about a team, we are talking neither about some monolithic faceless group nor about an assembly of value robots we can reprogram at will. Teams are composed of individuals, each with their own abilities, habits, tendencies, and attitudes. Once you sense that the organization and the individuals within it have decided to operationalize, the mindset is already changing for the better. At this point, it's imperative that you speed things up. You can't afford to linger too long before eliminating the old habits. Once a new, beneficial habit has taken hold, work hard to bury the old one.

During the change process, individuals will respond and embrace the change at different rates.

This is analogous to when a company launches a new product. It takes time for the product to gain traction and reach its sales potential. Taking a cue from the product life cycle, we can come up with a change life cycle and refer to people as adapters rather than adopters. This means your change efforts will cover the early adapters, the early majority, the late majority, and the laggards.

The early adapters are the pioneers who will switch immediately because they see the opportunity to make more money, to advance their career, or to play an important role in achieving a long-term goal. Whether they've participated in a value transformation before, or displayed adaptability in their previous roles, you need to identify them, support them, and, as far as possible, help them become evangelists for the transformation.

At the other end of spectrum you'll have the laggards, with the early and late majorities in between. It will be difficult to manage your systems with the laggards, so you have to make a distinction: who among the laggards is *struggling* to adapt, and who is *unwilling* to adapt? Keeping in mind that the pace of change will accelerate as new habits take hold and more people come onboard, the unwilling laggards can become a burden quickly unless they start to buy in. And that assumes only minor course corrections, never mind a market shock or significant unexpected change that puts everyone's adaptability to the test.

"All fixed set patterns are incapable of adaptability or pliability. The truth is outside of all fixed patterns."

Bruce Lee

Adaptability deserves recognition and reward

One way to accelerate change and encourage adaptability is to reward it. People who lead, pave the way, and pass on what they learn to encourage others play a valuable role in a transformation. As with anyone who produces superior value, these people and their acts should be recognized and rewarded. Even if the early adapters make mistakes, the organization benefits if the learnings from these failures make it easier for others to follow and adapt. These are the people who are thinking beyond the fixed patterns and the old ways of thinking.

This goes hand in hand with the change management idea of Emily Lawson and Colin Price that there are four conditions for changing mindsets:

Employees will alter their mind-sets only if they see the point of the change and agree with it— at least enough to give it a try. The surrounding structures (reward and recognition systems, for example) must be in tune with new behavior. Employees must have the skills to do what it requires. Finally, they must see people they respect modelling it actively.

The goal is to accelerate the adoption of these new ideas and processes by those employees in the early adapter and the early majority categories. If you do things correctly, they will adapt very quickly. As these early adapters buy in and talk about the change, this will prompt the late majority and eventually the lagging adapters to follow in turn. As organizational behaviorists Balazs and Kets de Vries stated in their manual of organization:

Individuals who feel alone in their efforts to change behavior patterns will have a difficult time changing.

That first step of adaptation is essential because those who are more likely to be in late majority, as well as the laggards, are watching the early major- ity group, learning from them, and watching their moves. They are deciding whether it is advantageous to make a change. They'll have numerous concerns and questions: Are we going to do it? Are we going to experiment? Are we going to start using the tools? If they see that the whole thing will likely be a tough process for them, they won't take the risk. If you show them that change is worth their while and offer them a smoother, battle-tested path to success, they are far more likely to have the right mindset and adapt.

It seems contradictory to say that you're rewarding people for making mistakes, but as we discussed in chapter 5, we have to be careful about how we describe failure. When your early adapters are debugging your new process, fixing the plan on the go, and keeping the existing machinery running as long as you still need it, they're amazing assets, not mistake-prone liabilities.

Motivating adaptation means making time for it

In the early stages of a transformation, we face mul- tiple challenges. The first is that you still have to do some things the old way until the new processes take hold and render the former ones (and the mindsets attached to them) obsolete.

That a value transformation takes time does not change the fact that time is our scarcest resource. Part of being adaptable is managing time and prioritizing on the go. Think back to the NASA reference at the beginning of this chapter. If we look at Apollo 13, the so-called successful failure and the subject of a major movie, we see how an organization shortened and sharpened its to-do list almost immediately, once the intermediate objective—landing on the moon—could no longer be met. The ultimate objective, however, remained the same: bringing all three astronauts home safely.

Now, of course, it's rare for a business to find itself in such sudden, life-or-death circumstances as the Apollo astronauts and Mission Control faced. The message here is not to create an artificial urgency, which would only add more stress. The message is that our priority lists are usually too long, filled with dubious items, and impossible to complete. This situation needs to change in general, not simply because you're undertaking a value transformation.

The solution to this challenge lies in how you communicate the importance of accomplishing each newly assigned task, such as completing a value journal and helping people learn to adapt, adjust, and narrow a priority list. You have to reinforce the entire value transformation idea, at both the leadership and the project team levels. Ensure that leaders at each level make time for people to experience and experiment with all the new ideas and processes being implemented. They must allow for a specified amount of time, such as an assigned half-hour or 45 minutes every Friday—or even every day—for employees to experiment on value. They can use this time to practice value messaging, complete value logs, or have internal or external value conversations. Or they can use the time to think and reflect.

This process will push employees into action mode. Other trainers and coaches around the world, including business trainer Cameron Morrissey, echo this sentiment:

> The key is to do follow up sessions to encourage dialogue, ensure compliance, and overcome obstacles. It is also a fantastic way to solicit further improvements. This could be every day after training, it could be every week afterwards, but the key to habit forming is repetition.

People should have time to experiment and try things without judgment or consequences. The goal is to create a comfort level. Think of it as practice or drills. You can promote adaptability and help people thrive when you create a safe zone: a place and time for people to play around with and experience change. At the same time, you must reduce the intricacy of the workload because people cannot deal with complexity on top of complexity.

It's a matter of changing both the existing processes and removing all unnecessary ties that inhibit learning. Even if it takes just six months, it's imperative for leaders to create space for those changes to occur.

Of course, this is easier said than done. Peoples' attitudes differ, and we've already spoken about the four different speeds at which people typically adapt. Leaders are no exception. Some management personnel you talk to may be too distant from the actual workload they assign to their subordinates. They'll give their employees more work, more tasks, and simply expect that they will find a way to do it. While this may be feasible to a certain extent with a very limited number of efficient, highly skilled workers, not everyone has the necessary management skills, organizational skills, and time management skills. Most people cannot effectively handle this workload and process the great change foisted upon them while completing their daily tasks. Ensure that leaders understand the importance of the value journey, and get them on board.

The secret recipe for improving adaptability

You can do all the right things, but you need to adjust and adapt over time. The secret ingredients to adaptability are incentives, resources (especially time and space), encouragement, and support.

Remember that the difference between value masters and value managers—or those who simply have good intentions—is execution. And proper execution will only happen if people are adaptable and have that space to experiment. They may have the talent, they may have the resources, they may have the tools, but they also need the time and the space.

All the above conditions influence and affect how people react and adapt to change. Creating these conditions and allowing your employees to flourish and grow is the only way your transformation will be successful and irreversible. The responsibility for creating these conditions lies with those in positions of authority and those who have been placed as value leaders on a team level.

We will dive further into this concept in the accountability chapter, where responsibility is paramount. But before that, we will look at alignment and discuss its value in determining just how successful the transformation will be.

Works Cited

Kets de Vries, Manfred F. R., and Katherina Balazs. *Transforming the Mind-Set of the Organization: An Owner's Manual.* Fontainebleau, France: INSEAD, 1996.

Lawson, Emily, and Colin Price. "The Psychology of Change Management." McKinsey Quarterly 2003 Special Edition: The Value in Organization, June 2003.

Morrissey, Cameron. "The Secret to Creating the Right Habits in Your Team." Cameronmorrissey.com, October 30, 2015, http://cameron-morrissey.com/blog/the-secret-to-creating-the-right-habits-in-your-team

Key learning

_____

_____

_____

_____

Key actions

_____

_____

_____

_____

7

A for Alignment

© LIOZU 2016

A LARGE COMPANY RECENTLY ASKED me to help them undertake a value transformation. During my initial assessment I asked what sounds like a simple question but immediately brings difficulties and conflicts to the surface: "What are your priorities today?"

The participants began listing what they believed to be their top tasks. I worked with them, and listened closely, but noticed two things that occur far too often when I ask that question at the beginning of a transformation. First, "value approach" and "value transformation" were nowhere to be seen on the lists. Second, the sheer number of priorities people have at any given time never ceases to amaze me.

When I approached the CEO and mentioned what seemed to be a breakdown in communication, I asked for clarification: "How do you expect people to work on sixteen strategic initiatives?"

That question may sound confrontational, but step back and think about it. Can a leader truly expect subordinates to cut their time sixteen different and often conflicting ways, above and beyond their existing daily processes? Can a leader then add new ideas and processes to the workload?

I recognized a massive lack of alignment between the CEO, the team, and the idea of value. At that time, he and I did not see a similar path for the future success of the company reflected in communication or in the match between abilities and actions on the ground level of the organization. Having a growth mindset is

"The task of leadership is to create an alignment of strengths so strong that it makes the system's weaknesses irrelevant."

Peter Drucker

not a matter of setting bold targets or adding tasks to people's responsibilities beyond their time, ability, or resources to satisfy them. A growth mindset requires an element of balance. Before we could initiate a successful value transformation, we needed to ensure proper alignment.

Alignment is not easy to achieve

Of course, who wouldn't want to have an entire organization pulling in one direction? Alignment sounds like an obvious goal with wonderful benefits. It sharpens the team's focus, concentrates its energies, and eliminates the time-consuming friction from internal conflicts.

But it's by no means simple.

Alignment is a multidimensional construct, comprising priorities, goals, incentives, processes, and actions. These are quite broad and sweeping labels, so as we move through our value transformation, we need to prioritize alignment itself as a critical path to success.

Every good manager knows that this is easier said than done.

Incentives play an important role

People will not emphasize value and pare down their priority lists without guidance from leadership. The right guidance helps employees prioritize certain tasks within their transformation that align with their own actions, attitudes, and abilities and those of others.

Most organizations will rightfully use incentives to achieve this. Rewards are important for motivation, but remember that too many objective incentives may cause an overload and lead to misalignment. There is a fine balancing act between incentivizing behavior and creating a system that people try to rig or game, thus putting their own self-interest far ahead of the organization's.

Perhaps the biggest fix here is to stop rewarding senior executives on profit or margin while rewarding salespeople for volume or revenue.

It's also worth remembering that successful alignment requires a cascade. From the CEO all the way down, there should be some overlap and continuity of goals, tasks, and rewards. The alignment must encompass all levels of the business, and the rewards must align with the goals. As reported in the *McKinsey Quarterly* article by Emily Lawson and Colin Price,

> Organizational designers broadly agree that reporting structures, management and operational processes, and measurement procedures— setting targets, measuring performance, and granting financial and nonfinancial rewards— must be consistent with the behavior that people are asked to embrace.

Organizations need to adhere to this goal-and-reward alignment from top to bottom. Everybody in the organization should be playing the same game under the same rules to reach the same end goal of the transformation. This goal might be gross margin improvement, value culture, profit, pricing improvements, or other common strategic goals. What's important is that everyone is working toward the same ends and receiving proportionate incentives to get there.

Common ground and the one-value vision

If you build such a program around value amid a growth mindset, you can unlock tremendous potential. This brings us to vision. I admit that the word gets overused and watered down. When I talk about

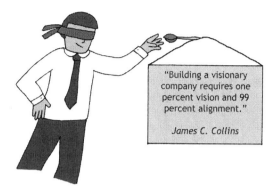

"Building a visionary company requires one percent vision and 99 percent alignment."

James C. Collins

vision, I'm thinking of the shared ideas that allow us to turn intangible goals—morale, success, value, growth—into tangible actions and results. It is your answer to the question "why?"

This commonality lies at the core of the value transformation journey. We're looking for a like-mindedness among the teams and the individuals within them. This like-mindedness grows from a convergence of views, language, systems, and so on. You cannot demand a like-minded team any more than you can mandate a growth mindset. But you can foster and nurture it.

Further down the hierarchy it becomes a much more complex, individual process. Managers need to help align their employees on things like language, common definitions, and interpretations. For instance, if all the employees come up with the same way of translating the customer's vocabulary during a dollarization exercise, the customer's feedback becomes something usable and valuable for them. They are aligned in their thinking and in how they get work done.

Training multifunctional groups plays a role here. As mentioned in chapter 4, this is the best way to help individuals adapt and align in their teams. As they work together in small groups, they begin thinking on a common level with a common thread. From this, they will begin creating common definitions, constructs, and visions of the concepts they're using and need to be using. They are building common ways of putting to use the tools they've been given. They are aligning organically in an environment you created.

Implementing the one-value vision

One of the best practices for fostering alignment organically is the idea of a *one-value vision* that everybody understands. Communicating the vision of the value transformation—and what value means to the organization—must be on the CEO's agenda and at the top of the agenda of each of your value leaders. The idea is to make everyone at all levels aware of the value transformation and the end goal. We have to anchor these concepts in every employee's brain, so that everyone intuitively knows how to turn intangibles into tangibles, and why that work matters.

Another important step is the creation of a value council. This council has an employee-driven focus and empowers each individual. It provides a safe place for groups to discuss value ideas and processes. They will give each other feedback about organizational actions and develop new processes and strategies. You are conditioning your employees to report the same way, using the same vocabulary. The teams come together and prioritize the same objectives, compile the same reports, and use the same project trackers. This reinforces the growing sense of alignment. It reinforces employee buy-in, creating positive attitudes toward transformation.

Talk is not enough, though. You need something to measure, to tie activities to results. I recommend a dashboard or tracker for critical value components or KPIs. Such dashboards have proved to be helpful in assessing the progress of the value transformation. You can discuss and compare the progress of the journey in value council meetings. By using a tracker, you can also record the number of times employees use the tools or concepts, to see immediately what's working and what may need more support or change.

I suggest that you hold these value council meetings quarterly, but there is no set frequency. I usually don't recommend monthly, because it imposes an extra workload with too little progress to measure. Your value team and project team leaders are already checking every month anyway, making sure transformation tasks are completed.

Mixing people matters

This approach is one of the strongest arguments against silos, "as needed" communication, and a general bias against sharing information. I have seen time and again that the more cross-functional, multi-functional, and multicultural work you do, the easier it will be for your company to align. We realize that our true commonalities are often much stronger than our perceived differences, once we do the necessary exploration. The more fluid and far-reaching the common perceptions, conceptions, and views among your workforce, the more comfortable your teams will be in interacting and helping each other.

There are no shortcuts on this end of the transformation. It will be time consuming. You will need a budget for travel and for extra, cross-functional training. You can use technology where possible, such as WebEx or videoconferencing. But ultimately there are benefits to natural interaction. It is sometimes a case of biting the bullet and investing in travel expenses for what I can assure you will be a fruitful exercise.

Employees on all levels have to be able to experiment and discuss their stakes together. They will exchange in advance, and they may also complain and moan and air their grievances. At the end, they will emerge all the better for it. This type of interaction and alignment creates confidence in the individuals and their teams. This confidence then bubbles up to affect relationships and processes across the company. This is another manifestation of one-value vision thinking.

You can rely on many techniques to create this snowball effect of alignment and confidence. The multifunctional sessions must be high energy and well prepared. Make sure that the exercises don't exclude anyone and that they slowly increase in complexity over time to maximize the learning process and the team's engagement. Before you know it, new value-driven processes will become second nature.

Giving new meaning to *go with the flow*

The more comfortable you are with your work and the more confident you are in your abilities, the easier it is for you to align and to adopt a value mindset. One prerequisite is a platform for change and the space to try it. Another prerequisite or condition is a training program that is highly engaging and that encourages experimentation. This means escaping the two-days-of-training-and-done approach and avoiding the check-the-boxes approach.

When I lead these training sessions, I often don't follow a set agenda. I'm more concerned with participants' views and degree of alignment and with the course of the discussion. I care about the bonds we're creating and the convergence of ideas we're facilitating, because this alignment drives the value transformation.

Within these sessions, I attempt to create and sustain a sense of excitement. The participants should lose a sense of time passing, because they're excited about what they're doing. It's the excitement created here that allows us to grasp and apply the full potential of these new methods. It's what the renowned psychologist Mihaly Csikszentmihalyi refers to as *flow*.

His research revealed that our mental state is a function of skill level and challenge. If both are at a high level, we can achieve flow, that feeling of immersion when we don't notice the passage of time and we see the achievement of the task as a reward unto itself. If both skill and challenge are at a low level, the result is apathy. Other mismatches of skill and challenge can lead to anxiety or boredom, whereas an alignment between skill and challenge can foster feelings of excitement and control.

This gives new meaning to the phrase *go with the flow*. It underscores why a growth mindset is so appealing compared with a fixed mindset. When we approach ability as something we can improve, and when we can align those skills with the challenges at hand, we can take on greater tasks, build momentum, and improve morale as well. These are key intangibles that drive the tangible actions and results we are pursuing.

Of course, to implement these changes we'll need to exchange some of our old ideas to remain aligned. Leaders and project managers need to make structural changes and redefine priorities so that we can increase convergence and flow.

This is not easy. Parting with past practices in exchange for an uncertain future is a tough trade-off. This is why we need change managers: to reduce uncertainty, create common ground, and establish an environment where alignment can grow organically. You need to have real coaches, people who can quickly

"Team alignment is the
constant fight against
perception gaps."

Stefano Mastrogiacomo

sense the alignment of a team and immediately modify approaches as needed. Great trainers will have
an empathetic sixth sense. They will sense the team
environment and dynamics and visualize the organizational alignment. Such coaches are critical to your
transformation.

To transform value,
you need collective role models

Role models are important in any organization. Seeing long-standing employees changing will influence
change in those seeking or needing mentorship. At
the same time, Lawson and Price observe,

> behavior in organizations is deeply affected not
> only by role models but also by the groups with
> which people identify.

So the idea of the role model extends past the individual to a group of individuals. You will have to pull all the strings at once, understand the room, and inspire change.

It takes just a few key people on a team to begin the transformation momentum you desire. Find these early adapters, reward them, and encourage them to drive alignment. These role models in the room, the ones who embrace change, supplement the work of the value coaches.

Working together, the coach and the role models serve as the center for alignment, attitude, and proficiency. They also carefully read the room during training and during day-to-day work. Are people getting it, or are they just nodding because they want to get out of there or move on? Are the employees engaged, or are they laggards who are stuck in their ways? Value transformations always require some heavy-duty, psychological, mental rewiring. You can create the environment for that to happen organically when you

- provide the right incentives
- reduce and sharpen priorities, with an emphasis on value
- find and reinforce commonalities, rather than yield to perceived differences
- answer the "why?" question, whether spoken or unspoken: define a one-value vision, which links our intangible goals and desires to tangible actions and results

- empathize with people's need for time to test, experiment, and grow comfortable and confident with new processes
- help people match their abilities to the organization's challenges . . . and then stretch both!
- align the training, too . . . the mix of coaches, role models, and mentors laying the groundwork for an easier journey by living out and exemplifying the alignment.

Works Cited

Lawson, Emily, and Colin Price. "The Psychology of Change Management." *McKinsey Quarterly 2003 Special Edition: The Value in Organization*, June 2003.

Key learning

_____

_____

_____

_____

Key actions

_____

_____

_____

_____

8

A for Accountability

YOU HEAR MANY SLOGANS today that have a link to accountability. From the Nike slogan "Just Do It" to the New England Patriots' mantra "Do Your Job" to the politically incorrect motto "Get Sh*t Done," many clarion calls urge us to accomplish our tasks at hand.

But as you've read many times in this book so far: easier said than done!

While I support and use each of those expressions above, accountability deserves a deeper exploration and a bigger context than we can pack into three-word slogans. Accountability is what makes an action-oriented culture also function as an accomplishment-oriented one.

Think for a moment what "do your job" might mean in your own context. I can tell you one thing. That saying does not permit the use of the excuse "that's not my job" when an unexpected situation arises. An accountable organization, made up of accountable people, is the antithesis of a silo organization where everyone follows instructions and keeps their head down.

In their book *Freedom, Inc.,* authors Brian M. Carney and Isaac Getz tell an anecdote about a customer who called his supplier at night because no one had picked him up at the airport. It was a true mix-up. This was in the days before cell phones, and the customer had had no chance prior to his arrival to alert the supplier to the change in his plans.

Christine, who was still in the office, answered the call, then took keys to a company car, picked up the

customer representative at the airport, and brought him to his hotel. After a 200-mile round trip, she returned to work and finished her duties without even telling anyone what had happened.

Why does this matter?

Christine was the cleaning lady.

Accountability is not a yes-or-no thing. It's a spectrum, and Christine is a shining example of the upper end of that spectrum.

The five shades of accountability

During a transformation, I like to use the same spectrum of accountability that I used in audits at my old job. It identifies five levels of accountability within an organization.

- **Level 1:** People expecting everything without contributing much in return.
- **Level 2:** Individual accountability regarding the work being done without considering how it fits into the overall environment.
- **Level 3:** Work unit or team accountability. It's a potential indicator of a silo organization.
- **Level 4:** Cross-functional accountability, where specific teams collaborate and accept the consequences of their work.
- **Level 5:** The entire organization working in harmony. This is the end goal—people working together, helping each other, and taking responsibility as a group.

You can imagine the distance and the effort that lie between level 1 and level 5! A value transformation should shift an organization from a system of do-nothing accountability to full organizational accountability. This means getting away from playing the blame game whereby sales blames marketing, marketing blames finance, and everyone blames sales. There's no place for finger pointing if you want to move forward. Everyone must work in the same direction and in support of each other.

If someone makes a mistake, they should raise their hand. We identify and clean up messes. And if we fail, we fail as a team.

Breaking down barriers to build accountability

It takes a seismic cultural change to move from individual accountability to a mindset where we all care as a team and each of our main goals is to question how the group can be more successful. This takes communication and confidence, all built in the previous stages of the process. It's now our leaders' responsibility to use these tools to break down the barriers that prevent personal and team accountability.

I've gone into companies that have tremendous workloads and equally tremendous communication barriers. How does anything meaningful ever get done over time?

The first task in addressing these situations is to break down all those barriers. The multifunctional work done in training as part of the transformation process fosters accountability because it instills individuals with the knowledge they need to collaborate to be successful. They need to own their mistakes in order to correct them. They learn how to do that by assessing their actions, successful or not, and discussing with colleagues how they can improve.

Remember that you project accountability to others

Can you imagine the reaction of a customer whose initial experience with your organization is observing varying levels of accountability? Listening between the lines, do they hear different degrees of "Yeah, I don't care," or do they get a sense of "Yes, I want my organization to be super successful"? The customer would see these different attitudes toward accountability, and that will have a strong halo effect on your value story. It can even undermine it. Remember, the value story is the whole reason for this transformation. It's the fulcrum that helps launch the organization to future success.

Now consider the alternative: each representative of the organization talking to the customer with the same sense of commitment, which conveys an energetic "If I fail, we all fail." They speak in one steadfast, focused voice. And they act like Christine did in the story above. This is where you see team spirit solidifying and confidence among your workforce blossoming.

Where does accountability begin?

This transition isn't easy. Above all, it requires top management to take the lead and hold themselves accountable. This is why my first step in addressing accountability is to ask a company's executives one simple question: "What are you going to do today to help this value transformation?"

Then I ask them to think about what happens if none of them has an answer. I stress the idea that accountability begins with them, at the top of the organizational pyramid. People watch what their

"Accountability separates the wishers in life from the action-takers that care enough about their future to account for their daily actions."

John Di Lemme

bosses, their leaders, do. Employees observing a lack of accountability at the top will say, "Well those guys didn't do it, so why should I?" So they return to, or continue to, practice business as usual. Executives and managers need to look at their own approaches, examine their commitment to the transformation, and assess their personal accountability. Then, and only then, will accountability flow throughout the organization.

Accountability is intrinsic to what we talked about in alignment, particularly in discussing the alignment of incentives. Succeeding at value transformation means tracking change explicitly and vigorously.

You will have your KPIs at the organizational level and at the individual level, as well as your financial KPIs and individual/change KPIs. Misalignment at these levels can become a barrier to growth.

Accountability means consequences . . . both positive and negative

The responsibility lies with management to put systems in place that incentivize and enforce accountability. How do you make sure people feel the pinch if they don't actually do the work, don't attempt to transform, don't change their attitude, don't adopt the tools they've been given, or don't show up to training?

Retired New England Patriots running back Kevin Faulk describes what accountability means to him in "The Patriot Way," a recent essay for *Player's Tribune*. We pick up the story as he frantically tries to arrive on time for a morning meeting:

So I finally arrived at the facility, pulled into the parking lot and threw the car into park. I don't even think I locked the doors. I just got out and hit the ground running, full sprint, through the snow, in slippers.

As I approached the building, I saw Coach Belichick walking into the meeting room, so I went around to check the back door. Thankfully, it was open, and I slid in the back way and into an open seat. By the time coach turned to address the team, I was sitting down, sweating, and pretending like nothing had happened.

Why the hustle to make a team meeting? Faulk knew that despite his own importance to the team's offense and special teams' success, missing a meeting meant a fine. Or worse. It could mean the loss of playing time. And ultimately it can cost a player his job.

My point here is not to praise the New England Patriots or to antagonize people who are not their fans. The point is that a lack of accountability must have personal consequences before it ever has a chance to have team and organizational consequences.

As a company transitions from a lower level on the spectrum to level 4 or level 5, money can make a difference. Before accountability becomes second nature, it needs to be treated as a form of merit and thus warrant merit-based rewards. For example, you might introduce an elemental pay incentive. Let the employees know that they won't be rewarded unless they thoroughly deserve to be. They need to understand that by not doing the work and dodging accountability, they're the ones who lose out. If they decide to not do something or not to buy in to something, then they will face the consequences.

As mentioned, leadership must use rewards like these wisely and align the rewards across the organization. They must reflect the organizational values and the value in each employee contributing to the transformation journey. At the individual level, you

can show that you value employees through performance reviews and evaluations. They can understand
how they're performing and see whether they're moving the needle on the dashboard tracker we discussed.
Then they can take the next step by asking themselves "What are the repercussions if I don't improve?
How can I get a merit increase and avoid a pay cut?"

My hope is that the need for these explicit rewards
diminishes as accountability improves and becomes
its own reward, as everyone has a chance to participate in an organization's success. But hope is not a
strategy, and we need to be practical in the meantime.

It makes sense to hold managers to the same levels
of accountability and give them same chances to be
incentivized. If you don't properly tie incentives, objectives, and priorities to performance reviews, you're not
going to move up the levels on overall accountability.

The role of human resources in accountability

One of the main players you need to get on board for
this transformation is human resources. It might be
difficult to get them excited about participating in a
value transformation project, however. A typical reaction from them is "Well, what am I supposed to do
there? It's all about pricing."

Explain to them the cross-functional and all-encom-
passing nature of value transformation. It will involve
improvements in internal communications, change
management, and entirely new types of training

programs. Critical aspects—from talent recruitment, development, and coaching, to mentoring and buddying, to things like role-playing—all warrant input and guidance from a professional human resources department. A value transformation will also alter job descriptions, modify performance reviews, and so on.

Facing the consequences

Here are some questions to ask before making big changes:

- What will these consequences be, especially toward the back end of the transformation?
- What are the consequences of you, your colleagues, or subordinates having a bad attitude and not adopting a change?
- If someone doesn't do the work, what consequences will they face?
- When there is a failure to adopt a change, do you let people go?

Consider the following scenario. For one year, as part of your old system, you rank individual sales based on volume. The next year, you rank the same people based on value and pricing. Will you hand down consequences for low performance? The top volume seller could be at the bottom of the ranking the next year if they don't buy into the new value stories and approaches you instill in your organization. How will you react, and what will you do to ensure that every-one in the organization adopts the new approaches and adapts?

If you lack accountability or if management fails to respond to nonperformance, your transformation will derail. A wholesale commitment to the transformation process across all levels and within all aspects of the organization is essential to its success. Adherence cannot be selective or optional.

Reconciling accountability with fairness

Accountability will inevitably become a key compe-tency for leadership and employees. It begins immedi-ately when you embed accountability metrics in your people processes and personnel review guidelines within the training program.

That statement and the consequences I described above may seem like authoritative leadership. But consider having five people who openly say "No, I'm not going to do it." That toxic behavior undermines the efforts of the entire organization and unleashes a contagious negative attitude. That is not theory. It happens, and I'm sure you've witnessed it.

You have options, but you need to choose among them and exercise them. Is the answer to fire these people, reassign them to another project, or perhaps stage an individual intervention where you lay out options for compliance? That depends on your organi-zation and the trade-offs you face. But the bottom line is this: if you don't enforce the principles you're trying to instill, you cannot foster accountability. And you must always lead by example.

But there's more to it than that.

Lack of accountability, or low levels of accountability, are not always due to misalignment and an intrinsic mindset. Claiming that is tantamount to claiming that mindsets are fixed. Have you looked at the potential for a growth mindset and created a path to it?

When assessing the performance of an employee who refuses to adapt, consider the root causes instead of taking the resistance or reluctance at face value and taking severe steps. Perhaps they're wrong for their current role and can contribute much more in a different role? If so, do they need to work on a different project? Do they need further training?

Or does the responsibility lie on your end as a leader or manager? Is your training or your communication making the problems worse instead of better?

No leader is infallible, and we have a responsibility to put people into roles and positions where they— and the organization—have the best chances of success. I believe in giving people a fair chance to adjust and allowing them as much time as you can afford to do so. I encourage you to look at where the problems are arising and try to solve them before resorting to dismissal. This is how you would remedy gaps in any other skill or competency. Perhaps you need to reassess your own?

The core message and the overarching objectives remain. All of this signals that you will not tolerate value mediocrity and nonperformance. You will, however, be fair, create opportunities to train everyone efficiently, and improve your own leadership skills to properly reinforce what you're trying to instill. You have to be logical and even-handed. Take the time to give people the space, training, and resources necessary for long-term success.

Remove the bottlenecks

You can have process bottlenecks and people bottlenecks. You need to understand the difference and act accordingly, in line with what we discussed in the previous sections. Despite your best efforts, a single person—no matter how impressive their other talents—can impede or even halt a transformation by preventing everyone below them from working together in the right direction. This person is often in a position that multiplies their disruptive effects on the process, even though it might not be intentional. You need to remove this blockage to allow the flow to resume. Counseling or firing one or two dissenters can unlock an organization's full potential and allow the value transformation to flow freely—an amazing thing to see happen!

Own your own accountability

Ultimately, accountability lies with you, the individual, before it moves to the team and organizational levels. Where are you right now on the spectrum of accountability that I introduced at the start of the chapter? Here are some deeper questions we can ask ourselves at the outset of a transformation:

- Are we individually accountable?
- Are teams already accountable?
- Are they working together?
- Are they watching each other's backs, or are they operating under an "every person for him- or herself" mentality?

Track every action and define the key terms of this transformation for the team you're working with. Displaying and sticking to this team mentality is especially important in front of your customers. Show them that all your employees and/or teammates share the same values and are working toward the same ends.

During a transformation, train everybody on what accountability means and how to assess both their current status and where they need to be. Teach people how to perform self-diagnostics.

I often go into a transformation and tell everybody where we need to be in three years. I outline how we're going to do it: multifunctional themes, a lot of project work together, and rewiring a great deal of the language. In addition to all that, we will each stand up and be accountable for our actions. That means accepting the consequences of not completing tasks to the best of our ability, and reaping the rewards when we do.

Works Cited

Carney, Brian M., and Isaac Getz. *Freedom, Inc.: Free Your Employees and Let Them Lead Your Business to Higher Productivity, Profits, and Growth.* New York: Crown Business, 2009.

Faulk, Kevin. "The Patriot Way." *The Players' Tribune,* January 13, 2017, https://www.theplayerstribune.com /kevin-faulk-patriots-way/.

Liozu, Stephan. "A Culture of Accountability: Five Tips for Developing Accountability So the Entire Organization Works in Concert." *Smart Business Pittsburgh,* October 2014.

Key learning

_____

_____

_____

_____

Key actions

_____

_____

_____

_____

9

Best Practices
for Training Excellence

© LIOZU 2017

B Y NOW YOU'VE NOTICED that training is the engine of the whole value transformation. Training is how we establish a growth mindset built on the six As. It's how we impart the organization's new vision, objectives, concepts, approaches, and tools to each rank-and-file employee, to each team, and to each executive throughout the business. Your company deserves this investment in dedicated training.

At the same time, how do we distill and pass along best practices for training when every business is different? Differences in scope, culture, and market mean that every training program requires customization. Meeting that challenge isn't easy, but it brings great rewards. You will have more dedicated, aligned, productive employees who see that you've invested in their futures.

Fortunately, there's a method to the apparent madness.

Despite—or perhaps because of—this demand for customized training, I've developed a list of training best practices that can help you achieve the results your team and organization expect and deserve. These lessons are based on my career of initiating value transformations, coaching people in organizations across the world, and helping them take advantage of new tools and ideas as well as old ones they already have access to.

Our goal is to train and retrain, constantly checking in with individuals to reinforce the values of the hard work done in the original training. Remember that the point of this transformation is to better ourselves and our performance, individually and as an organization.

Step 1: Rethink how training works

Let's be realistic about the scope here. We will be training many different people on many different things. This cannot occur overnight; nor can it occur using conventional methods. The best practice model we will use is instead a total redesign of the traditional lecture-class approach. We have to stop carpet-bombing people with information, then releasing them back to their own devices to sink or swim. Feedback and follow-up are critical.

Instead of relying on day-long lectures, begin with a formal training session. Training will take place over three to six or even twelve months, during which time we will collect multiple data points and have multiple contacts with each trainee. In reality, training never stops, because the value transformation never stops. The roadmap needs to account for many touch points of reinforcement. New people will come and go in your organization, making frequent training blitzes necessary.

Step 2: Plan and create a roadmap

Over time and on a regular schedule, the trainer must touch base with the trainees. To ensure that you stay on schedule, first design a rough draft with a timeline for your training. Then create a list of touch points. Before you attempt to merge these tools into a road-map, create a template or a document for this road-map in simple spreadsheet software. List the weeks along the top and the touch points along the side.

To devise the schedule, start by listing things like in-house obligations that can help you define available time. You will need to account for webinars, monthly meetings, weekly sales calls, email blasts, text campaign, daily reminders, and so forth. With these in mind, you can map out when the training (and the transformation steps) can actually occur. This will help you set a schedule and identify the formats you might follow.

The touch points for follow-up will reinforce the initial training content. The number of touch points is very important, and the motto is "the more, the better." You're not trying to minimize or optimize the number of touch points right now. The objective is to make the content stick. Saturation and the constant backing up of this knowledge are crucial. I recommend having ten touch points with each trainee in a space of three to six weeks after an original presentation of material. This is much stronger reinforcement than what you achieve over the span of two hours at a conference.

To keep these ten touch points from becoming a monotonous burden, it is essential to include a mix of delivery methods in your roadmap, including virtual

"Becoming is better than being."

Carol Dweck

and in-person methods, as well as hybrid forms. Watch a video in a classroom, then get out of your seats and complete an exercise based on the information presented. You may also have multiple trainers connecting to a single platform, using their different coaching skills at a single point. Maybe you can use something as simple as a phone call plus matching video. No matter how you perform the task, the key to absorption is to engage trainees over the space of three to six months. Use all available technologies at your disposal, and be creative.

Step 3: Get the blend of methods right

Flexibility is essential to finding the right blend of methods for successful transformation training. With today's ever-increasing levels of technology and globalization, you can't just expect to have all the people you need together in a room whenever you need them. Apart from an initial meeting, it may be logistically impossible to get the entire group together again. You have to find alternative approaches.

We have to diversify and be flexible in our delivery methods. As their coach and leader, you have to touch base with them any way you can and avoid using technology or timing as an excuse. Whatever the method, proper use of time is essential to achieving the most touch points possible in the time provided.

Think beyond traditional methods and look for openings in people's schedules. Maybe you take advantage of something as simple as a layover between flights for a quick trainer call. Or you record podcasts for trainees to listen to on a commute. Take advantage of local team meetings or gatherings to have peer discussions on value. There are many options to weigh and leverage without waiting for a conventional two-hour meeting next time they are in town or trying to wedge a full-day workshop into people's busy lives.

You also need to vary the style and voice of your follow-ups. This is another reason why we need to have several people involved as leaders, coaches, and trainers. You cannot have the same person giving the

entire training over a period of months. People need variety to maintain focus and absorb information. Here you can look to internal options first. There is no reason why every level can't participate, from the CEO down to the trainees' peers.

We are using the available time of all these opinion leaders to make sure we deliver the messages consistently. You can use an external coach or trainer to deliver the initial message or concept, but the best follow-up is constant reinforcement from within. Include managers, some coaches, executives, value experts, direct supervisors, and peers. Peers should not be just any peers; they should be value leaders themselves, well versed in your value message and ideally having performed a similar task in a previous job. These individuals are perfect to deliver messages and training.

You might be surprised by the number of people in your organization who are value experts!

In my many training experiences, especially at large companies, I always find several people in a group who received recognition for "best in class" training at some point in their lives. These individuals are everywhere, and their value experience can offer you a massive boost in training other employees. Even better, they will often be eager to assist and spread their positive attitude. This is very valuable when motivating others to commit. Identifying these individuals early in the planning process is important. Often all you need to do is ask a few simple direct questions to see if people do have any experience.

One unbeatable advantage these peers can have is their ability to tell a story about their previous successes. They can share the pragmatic pains and gains of their journey. Storytelling is now in vogue as a training approach, and it should be an important form of training in any extensive, broad-based program. The stories these individuals can share of their own transformation will add a personal touch to the journey. It gives their peers something to identify with and commit to. It gives them hope that it can be done. Hope, in turn, brings confidence to take action. If you have all these value managers eager to share their story, why not use them to your advantage?

Storytelling and training approaches do not always need to come from within, though. To supplement your own value leaders, you can get creative here as well. Retired executives, professional athletes, coaches, military veterans, and even your own customers and suppliers can add invaluable insights to the content you want to convey and do it in a way no classroom teacher ever could.

You can also use online resources and platforms to supplement your own approaches and stories.

"Make sense with stories. If you give people facts without a story, they will explain it within their existing belief system. The best way to promote a new or different belief is not with facts, but with a story."

David Gray

Online cloud platforms encourage ad hoc interaction, which can be valuable far beyond your planned training. They offer file and slide sharing whereby colleagues can interact and offer each other advice and feedback. They can also connect them with their trainers and coaches. We can't capture these touch points on our roadmap in advance, because they are spontaneous and help new internal networks grow organically.

You can also tap into websites with reinforcement training. One such site is Khan Academy, a nonprofit educational organization created in 2006 by educator Salman Khan with the goal of creating an accessible place for people to learn. The organization produces short lectures in the form of YouTube videos on a broad range of topics. Its website also includes supplementary practice exercises and tools for educators. This is just one example of a tool that could be set up internally to add extra touch points.

Step 4: Work to help each person absorb the material

Think about how you might help your kids when they're doing their homework, or how teachers are trained to differentiate between students of varying ability. They must deliver the same subject, the same topic, but must work harder with some students to make sure they absorb the material. They figure out a blend of techniques over time with concepts that resonate best with the individual student. They must make the material relevant and interesting.

Why should the business world be any different?

To get an organization of diverse individuals absorbing and embodying the same ideas is challenging, but not impossible. Each person learns differently, and each may be captivated by different things. They may even have different capacities to process information, sometimes referred to in academia as *absorptive capacity.* We want to transform mindsets and get people into transformational change mode. Start simply and increase complexity over time. You don't want to overwhelm people with too much work. We want to make sure the knowledge they're getting is going to stick, and there are proven and universal best practices we can capitalize on. Here is my basic approach to concepts and application before I begin adapting and customizing:

- **Start with a 50/50 mix:** In the first wave, present 50 percent exercises and 50 percent concepts. The concepts are delivered like emails, tips, little tidbits to read, training, and ideas.
- **Aim later for an 80/20 mix:** As you progress in the transformation, 80 percent will be exercises and 20 percent will be concepts.
- **Then continue with 100 percent coaching for reinforcement over time, focusing on those who are a bit behind.**

- **Keep it relevant:** Deliver concepts that are relevant to people's daily work and not theoretical. This is one of the most important filters you have.
- **Experiment:** One exercise I've used effectively is speed role-playing, where you give the audience a little exercise and within five minutes they have to role-play it.
- **Play and test:** Have the trainees role-play using the value tools. These skills will be directly transferable and critical to reinforce.
- **Help people feel comfortable:** During role-play exercises, no supervisors should be in the room with subordinates. The idea is to create a comfort zone.
- **Have fun:** You can't be serious or intense all the time.

The point of these exercises is to create confidence in the processes and between colleagues. I've even done a stomach bump competition in one program. I set up a jury and we awarded prizes to the winners. This event had nothing to do with value but allowed the participants to bond. It also allowed them to relax. You cannot expect to keep the trainees serious and under pressure. You want them to want to be there!

Even with this approach, you can still lose your trainees if you making sticking to a strict agenda your priority. You have to be agile and flexible. When I lead training, if I see something working well, I may adjust to encompass more of this successful aspect. If something isn't working, I may change the agenda, delay some point, or even cancel a section if necessary. So the priority is group flow and collective confidence. It's less about sticking to the agenda or about trainer's ratings.

Ultimately, collaboration and cooperation keep interest alive and speed absorption. This applies to the team and also to the coach with the group. Having that intimacy and that bond is much more important than following the preplanned agenda religiously. You're building lasting confidence and a sense of trust. Your agility in setting up these training programs and in modifying them reinforces that your focus is on the trainees and their welfare and progress, not on your agenda.

Summarizing the training best practices for value mindsets and value transformation:

Let's review the best practices for training to a value mindset and a value transformation.

- **Plan on at least ten touch points:** Conventional classroom instruction is not sufficient, and face-to-face follow-up is often impractical in our global world. You have to reconnect, the more frequently the better.
- **Mix delivery methods:** Transmit your methods virtually, physically, or as a hybrid.

- **Mix up your training environment:** Training can occur in a classroom or in the field, at home, or even in the car.
- **Use your value leaders:** The individual reinforcing the message can be a manager, coach, team leader, or peer. Each may have a success story to tell.
- **Account for different absorption levels:** Some learn best from seeing, others from reading, doing, listening, or taking actions.
- **Trainers and coaches must energize the teams:** Energy and positive attitude levels must be significant and genuine. Teams should feel exhausted at the end of each day.

Now it's time for our own final touch point. The key point from this chapter—perhaps this entire book—is that training is now about knowledge delivery: a vigorous, never-ending exchange among multiple trainees and trainers. It's not about conventional lectures and workshops. Training is a continual commitment, and there is no longer time for excuses.

You will get out of the value transformation what you put into it. We're doing a lot of rewiring, not only creating new connections for these individuals but rewiring the brain. We're systemically altering belief systems and instilling a mindset based on growth. We're building their confidence and giving them the platform to succeed. Success stories are essential, from peers, from people who have experienced transformation, and from the organization's application of their new knowledge, tools, and techniques.

We must all increase the openness of everyone in the organization, urge them to commit, pique their interest, and sustain the transformation. Be the change you want to see in your colleagues.

Key learning

_____

_____

_____

_____

Key actions

_____

_____

_____

_____

10

When and How
Do You Get Started?

© LIOZU 2016

THE PROSPECT OF GEARING up and beginning a value transformation can be daunting. I've seen this apprehension expressed many times with many different clients. In every case, the client has already recognized the need for the organization to undergo a value transformation. And as you know after reading this far, mindset must be a primary focus if the transformation is to be successful and irreversible. Every transformation begins with, builds from, and promotes that value mindset.

Yet the question remains: How does the organization get started?

The challenge is to turn something perceived as daunting into something the organization can visualize as exciting, rewarding, and, above all, achievable. That is clearly a mindset challenge. As the saying goes, the journey begins with a first step, and the first step of a value transformation—broadly speaking—is preparation. More specifically, it means defining success. It also means putting the pieces in place which I summarize below in my five tips for creating a value mindset:

1 Align around a **value dashboard** with clear metrics.
2 Provide specific **daily practices** to improve value abilities.
3 Accumulate and communicate **evidence of success**!
4 Praise for **efforts**, accomplishments, perseverance, and personal investment.
5 Focus on **personal transformation** by changing people's beliefs and inner narratives.

In the rest of this chapter I elaborate on each of these tips so that you can easily see how you can apply them to your own organization: what is your vision for success, and what is your best path toward achieving it?

Building *personal* change to create *collective* change

The bolded keywords and terms in the five tips form the foundation on which we will build and perform our transformation. Implementing and then sticking to these conditions will generate a roadmap of transformation. Turn each tip into a question and come up with the most precise answers you can for the moment. This process begins, again, with defining success. You cannot prepare a value dashboard and establish metrics—both quantitative and qualitative—unless you know what you're trying to accomplish and you let that vision and definition of success guide you.

This thought process, in turn, makes it easy to plan our journey in such a way that incorporates not only a very strong change management character but also a mindset transformation character. You travel this journey by implementing the six As, which you should be very familiar with by now.

The key objective becomes not only an organizational transformation but a personal transformation as well. You'll end up changing people's beliefs. You may change which leaders they see as role models and which people they themselves can inspire and encourage through their successes.

Step 1: The value dashboard

Let's take a deeper look at the five tips listed above. The first one, the value dashboard, is critical to showing people that they're making progress, both individually and collectively. If you can't demonstrate that you're moving forward with your transformation, then it's going to be very difficult to convince others that it's working. Your change management dashboard needs to include a way to track what's working and progressing.

Establish a clear qualitative and quantitative matrix. You can also use your tracker or dashboard to do this. Use it to measure the development of your journey and the tasks set out on your dashboard, then track it every three to six months. Of course, the exact time period is at your discretion. The important thing is to monitor the proverbial needle and ensure that it's moving toward success.

Incorporating quantitative and qualitative KPIs in your dashboard is essential. Remember that the qualitative KPIs often reflect mindset change. Change typically happens when people see other people use the tools properly and apply the skills you've provided, and as we will discuss in detail later, you need a way to capture efforts, perseverance, resilience, and other markers of a positive value mindset.

The qualitative side is crucial to the transformation because the progress is not composed solely of the movement of numbers. It also requires movement in morale and in employee satisfaction. If you have crappy morale and good numbers, it means people are just going to be cranking the numbers out. You may have some successes, but not irreversible ones. Any progress will be short-term and won't stick.

While you cannot constantly observe people doing their work, you can encourage them to keep a value journal. These can be a valuable input for the dashboard. Collect the journals and review them weekly.

This needs to be a self-encouraged exercise. You may encounter some opposition in using self-recorded data to justify progress. But it's something you can show top management to demonstrate that the transformation's working or, if it's not, to determine how to fix it. It will aid in measuring and assessing whether people are changing their approach to and attitude toward value.

I refer to this as the underside of the transformation, and if we don't manage the underside of the transformation, we don't know if the entire process will work.

Peter Drucker's message perfectly captures the need to measure and keep track of our journey's progress. If you fail to recognize that something

"What gets measured, gets managed."

Peter Drucker

isn't working, you can't fix it. If you fail to recognize that something is succeeding, you can't communicate the success in an effort to praise your team and bring the late adapters and laggards on board.

Find a way to give equal attention to both the qualitative side and the hard-numbers side of progress toward success. Many transformations neglect the human side of the transformation and fail. If you follow my process and instructions, you'll avoid that mistake.

Step 2: Daily practices:
Adjust, realign, and adjust again

If you want to evolve your traditional training roadmap into a true roadmap for knowledge delivery, you need a means of reinforcement. That means helping your team develop daily habits. While I emphasize again that you cannot overwhelm people, you also need to help them understand that value transformation is a long journey that requires constant attention and care. It is not a time filler, nor is it a set of boxes to check, or an occasional retreat from day-to-day work.

You have to focus on daily practices over time, but you also need to be fair to the teams. This means that the leaders must

- ensure that everyone has received the proper resources
- redesign the budget based on that information

- list the inventory of technology used, such as webcasts or podcast webinars
- leverage every single bit of technology available.

By resources, I do not mean simply making tools available. That is not sufficient. It's wishful thinking to believe that having access to tools automatically leads to their use. Tools without education, encouragement, and monitoring are a waste of time.

Reinforcement can take place in a structured or even in an ad hoc way, as I mentioned in previous chapters. You don't need to make a huge science

"A fool with a tool is still a fool."

Grady Booch

project out of it. You're clearly on the right path when you can have open conversations based on these simple questions:

- What daily tasks are you undertaking to motivate on value?
- How do you impact customer value every day?
- How are you making value a strategic priority?

These questions are enough to start a fruitful conversation.

Step 3: Success, success, success—Bang the drum!

Success breeds confidence. And confidence breeds success. I've stressed those points in previous transformations that I've helped companies undertake as well as in books I've written.

This cycle of success and confidence feeds off positive outcomes. As the value dashboard and the training roadmap take hold, you will witness stories emerging throughout the organization. Documenting these qualitative and quantitative stories, first daily and then monthly, will give you a storehouse of material you can use to inspire people. Remember, we're trying to turn what's perceived as a daunting task into one that's exciting, rewarding, and, above all, achievable. These success stories show people that progress doesn't have to mean moving huge mountains or reaching massive milestones. You should also bang the drum for the little nuggets. The smallest of achievements or victories are still wins and may be just the final piece someone needs to build their own momentum.

Success here is not only defined by something as narrow as a price increase you've implemented. That, of course, is an important outcome! But what makes a transformation stick is the practice of continuously striving for favorable outcomes and positive practices. Implementing a new training system, successfully using your journal to track the transformation, or finding a new way to satisfy a customer are perfect examples of small, personal accomplishments that make a difference. An employee can be proud of any of those achievements. They can say "I did that. I showed them our differentiation and they placed an order for five truckloads." The idea is to nurture this pride in the workplace and confidence in your colleagues until it saturates your organization.

You should immediately begin internally tracking past and current success stories. Past stories can play a vital role because they honor your team's previous accomplishments and avoid the impression that a goal of the transformation is to invalidate all past practices and successes. A value transformation is not a black-and-white, night-and-day, either-or repudiation of the past. The real world is never that clear-cut.

The more you demonstrate success, the more confidence you'll build at the individual and collective levels. Success stories and lessons will breathe new confidence into the organization very quickly. You should use all channels of communication, formal and informal, to spread the word. You can also institution-alize stories in your training programs, as you have internal champions show how things get done. They embody the success stories. Having them onboard is essential to building confidence and trust from day one.

Step 4: Carrots are still mightier than sticks

You might recall my citing Jedi master Yoda in chapter 4: "Do, or do not. There is no try."

Obviously, no transformation will succeed without concrete improvement and better outcomes. You have to remain results-driven, but you cannot be results-driven unless you are also effort-driven. We work hard, we learn from failures, and we realize that we might not be able to shout "done!" the very first time.

So what do you do with someone who puts in a lot of effort? You reward them.

To this end, my fourth tip requires examining the culture of performance within your organization. How do you define performance? Is performance defined only through outright success, or do things like effort and perseverance count? In my opinion, those intangibles absolutely do count!

During the transformation, you improve your chances for success if you adopt a vocabulary that encourages and offers higher praise for people's efforts. This new vocabulary should be one of the key differences between the old organization's structure and the new, transformed one. This differentiation is paramount.

Praising people for their perseverance, resilience, and personal investment strengthens their morale and work ethic. This matters, because advancing any transformation will be difficult. It's a laborious process. We're working with results in mind as well as concern for attitude and effort. We also need to account for the degree of difficulty in some tasks and place performance in that context. It's about finding the proper balance.

I remember a personnel review when I was working for a German company in 2006. One dimension of performance was attitude. If you had a very good level of attitude and showed a corresponding level of effort but failed to make your quota, you were not penalized. Please keep this in perspective. The goal is not to let everyone off the hook and create a culture where missing quotas is de rigueur. The expectation is that a positive attitude, coupled with appropriate action, will eventually lead to accomplishment. You have to keep people on track in the meantime.

One step you can take is to incentivize your employees on different dimensions, such as effort, resilience, and attitude. This shifts the focus from an all-out pursuit of numbers and targets. When we train, it is essential that we recognize everyone's efforts and don't only applaud the champions. This approach acknowledges that some colleagues face tremendously challenging market conditions within some regions, or confront a great deal of competition, and still manage to make progress. This is what I mean by acknowledging degree of difficulty. You need to assess and categorize the effort fairly and spread praise and rewards accordingly.

Problems may occur wherever teams are consistently falling short of targets. Personally, I don't like to penalize someone who has a great attitude, exhibits great effort and resilience, but fails to meet half their objective. Where effort is shown, improvement will follow, and people can eventually achieve higher performance. So, some employees will need you to help them find out what's going on.

This approach also helps a company avoid a culture of low expectations and create one that is willing—and eventually able—to meet very audacious goals. I recall the words of Michelangelo here:

The greater danger for most of us lies not in setting our aim too high and falling short; but in setting our aim too low, and achieving our mark.

A variety of factors may impact someone's business performance. They may lag behind but be willing to work. That attitude is key. Your value champions and managers will have a big part to play here. The people who have that great attitude and those appealing, highly attuned traits of effort, resilience, and drive have the best potential to develop into high performers. Ultimately they will drive your transformation and help others reach their own potential.

Step 5: Focus on the personal and the collective will follow

Prosci Change Management affirms that organizational transformation is really a series of individual transformations. If you want to effect change management at the collective level, you have to begin change management at the individual level. The same is true with a value transformation. If you want to transform 100 people, you'll have to bring those people on board one by one.

Doing this requires the full involvement of human resources. That entails coaching, peer development, mentoring, shadowing, and all those key subprocesses in the people management process. Human resources teams are important for internal communication and must have a central role. They should also help drive changes to review processes, objectives, job descriptions, roles, and responsibilities of many employees.

This works best with the help of people who professionally manage personnel and resources. They can best help you design a process that is flexible, agile, customized, and tailored to certain individuals or types of individuals to suit their needs. This will help those individuals embrace and connect to the transformation. This is what changes the inner narrative in the company, on the underside, one person at a time.

* * *

© LIOZU 2016

In this chapter we've covered in depth the elements necessary to begin a transformation. You have thought—correctly!—that these are also the five steps necessary to continue and complete a transformation. They must be reviewed, implemented, re-evaluated, and used continuously throughout the transformation. In essence, the process never ends. The value mindset must become ingrained in the culture and operations of the organization. As new people join the teams and changes occur in the business, you'll have to constantly measure and reassess.

I strongly encourage you to have your employees take the value mindset assessment included in the Resources section of this book at regular intervals to see where they stand. Every time you have a meeting related to value transformation, for example, end it by asking those present to take the assessment and discuss their reactions. It's a quick and concise way to open up a valuable dialogue and answer important questions: What do we need to? What's preventing us from moving as fast as we should be? And always remember the six-A model that serves as our reference point.

Any company can embark on a value transformation. They all have access to the tools, the methods, the books, and great consultants. The difference between those who are stuck in the zone of good intentions and those who move ahead is MINDSET. A value mindset is not sharable, transferable, or imitable. You have to find your own and own it. It's developed over time, and it can become a true competitive advantage. A value mindset makes companies value masters. There are only a few around. Your company can also become one. Be bold. Join the value revolution!

Key learning

_____

_____

_____

_____

Key actions

_____

_____

_____

_____

Resources

This section provides you with some of the tools I've used in many of my value transformation projects. Even if these aren't relevant to your business or project, you might find one or two nuggets to make your projects better. The lists of tools and actions are in no way exhaustive.

A. Value actions for account and sales managers

1 Communicating *daily* value messages (vision, brand message, differentiation)
2 Memorizing and delivering critical value messages ("Did you know?") (*daily*)
3 Having prepared value conversations with accounts (*quarterly*)
4 Asking specific value questions to support value-data collection drive (*weekly* value discovery drive)
5 Working on personal value action plan (*weekly*)
6 Populating the weekly value log or value journal (*daily*)
7 Maintaining value scorecard and working on it jointly with accounts (*weekly*)
8 Spending 30 to 45 minutes *daily* on value-selling actions and activities (preparing visits, listing questions, updating documents, reading value best practices, creating best practices, etc.)
9 Calling value coaches supporting your territory or business unit with specific questions, needs, or ideas (staying engaged) (*monthly*)
10 Identifying and engaging a value buddy on the team to share experiences, wins, challenges (*monthly*)
11 Working on the dollarization of a product or service (refreshing, starting, collecting, or validating data) (*monthly*)
12 Entering value information for specific accounts into CRM system (*daily*)

13 Refreshing the customer value file before visiting an account (*daily*)

14 Training dealer's sales staff on the value script for product and services (*daily*)

15 Writing value case studies or success stories (*monthly*)

16 Spending one day a month selling value to end users or consumers (*monthly*)

17 Engaging a community on WhatsApp or Viber with specific value messages (*daily*)

18 Volunteering to experiment and test new value propositions and value models (*quarterly*)

19 Documenting value interactions with accounts and entering the information into the account plans (*daily*)

20 Validating intentionally that customers belong to the right segments (proactively communicating with the marketing team) (*daily*)

21 Learning to talk about margins and less about prices using the Margin Tool (*ongoing*)

22 Giving regular feedback about the value tools to marketing team (*ongoing*)

23 Proactively identifying uncovered and hidden needs of dealers for new sell-out programs (*ongoing*)

24 Documenting and communicating pricing objections and value responses (*weekly*)

25 Using value calculators in front of customers to teach and convince (*daily*)

B. Value actions for top executives or leaders

1 Communicating *daily* value messages (vision, brand message, differentiation)
2 Reinforcing the need for change and vision for value (*daily*)
3 Setting priorities for teams involved in the value approach (*quarterly*)
4 Aligning compensation plans and objectives in the business unit and territories (*ongoing*)
5 Holding regular one-on-one meetings on the value transformation with middle managers (country manager, marketing manager, plant leader, etc.) (*monthly*)
6 Holding innovation brainstorming sessions to support value breakthrough actions for services, SCM, short-term blitzes (*quarterly*)
7 Attending territory and regional value council meetings (*quarterly*)
8 Systematic messaging from the top at all opportunities possible: Passion for value (*daily*)
9 Meeting proactively with value project team or value team (*monthly*)
10 Taking regional or divisional value ambassadors to lunch for a debrief and for support (*monthly*)
11 Visiting strategic accounts during launch period of value-based approach (fleets, value buyers, large accounts, early adopters) (*quarterly*)
12 Getting CVM® certified and participating in dollarization exercises (*quarterly*)

13 Calling one or two value champions each week for support (*weekly*)

14 Starting every staff and/or department meeting with key message on value (vision, approach, differentiation, etc.) (*weekly or monthly*)

15 Organizing Lunch with the Leader to discuss customer value (*monthly*)

16 Spending time in distributor location to learn how to sell value (*quarterly*)

17 Promoting win and success stories internally to build confidence (*daily*)

18 Joining important value kick-off meetings (planned or unplanned) (*monthly*)

19 Solving complexity and resource bottlenecks in a timely fashion (*ongoing*)

20 Technical function: Visiting distributors and value sellers in the field (*quarterly*)

21 Technical function: Training teams on essentials of the value approach (plants, labs, etc.) (*quarterly*)

22 Becoming fluent in the key pillars of the value approach: segmentation, differentiation, value (*ongoing*)

23 Visiting remote plants and offices to explain the importance of customer value (*quarterly*)

24 Enabling training of central teams on the value approach (finance, SCM, technical) (*ongoing*)

25 Providing reactive, fast, and timely support for sensitive and strategic deals (*ongoing*)

C. Value-based marketing tools

1 Value scorecard (value selling)
2 Customer value file (value selling)
3 Personal value journal (value mindset)
4 Value booklet or passport (value selling)
5 Internal value success stories (value selling & mindset)
6 Internal customer value proposition (value selling & mindset)
7 Internal value model / dollarization template (EVE®) (value selling)
8 External customer value proposition (value selling & communication)
9 Dollarized value bulletins (value selling & communication)
10 Dollarized application profiles (value selling & communication)
11 Value message list (value selling & communication)
12 "Value topic of the month" program (value selling & communication)
13 Value scripts for dealers for end users (value selling & training)
14 Value scripts for dealers against their local competitors (value communication)
15 Value Q&A or FAQs
16 Pricing objection management guide (negotiation for value)

17 Value video on YouTube (value selling & communication)

18 Dedicated value YouTube channel (value-based marketing)

19 List of value power words (value mindset)

20 Dramatic statistics for value ("Did you know?" series) (value selling & communication)

21 Internal value vision & roadmap (value mindset)

22 Value management dashboard (value mindset)

23 Personal value action plan for account managers (value mindset)

24 Value simulators or app for end users (value selling & communication)

25 Value digital kit (tweets, QR quotes) (value-based marketing)

26 Value invoice (no charge) (value selling & communication)

27 Customer value stories (value selling & communication)

28 Value quotes from top management (value communication)

29 Value videos from top management (value communication)

30 Value audit framework (for customer or distributor) (value selling)

31 Value testimonial letters (value selling & communication)

32 Value community (value mindset)

33 Dealer & consumer value events (value selling & communication)

34 Value-specific dealer/consumer survey (value discovery)

35 Internal value positioning maps (value-based marketing)

36 Customer value delivery deliverable for Stage-Gate® (value-based innovation)

37 Product calculators (for key performance drivers) (value-based marketing)

38 Customer segmentation quick guide ("how to" quick qualification process) (value-based selling)

39 Pocket value guide for sales teams and dealer's sales staff (value-based marketing)

40 Video game simulator or other fun activity (value-based marketing)

41 "Value Board Game" to practice and learn dollarization with end users (value-based selling)

42 Value tour in plants, offices, and any remote location (value communication)

43 Monthly value newsletter (internal or external) (value communication)

44 Salesforce margin tool (value-based selling)

45 Price/volume calculator/simulator for dealer to show dramatic impact of discounting (value-based marketing)

46 Customer-facing toolkit for salesforce (value-based selling and communication)

47 Value of brand stories (value communication)

48 Ease to use and deploy digital kit for partners and dealers (value-based marketing)

49 Consumer/dealer annual value awards (value communication)

50 Value-partner private events as part of a road-show or dedicated (value-based marketing)

51 Value brainstorming process kit to be used by dealers and partners (how to differentiate yourself from your competition) (value-based innovation)

52 Value and pricing comics (value communication)

53 Value-based loyalty program and club (value-based marketing)

54 Value lunches with dealer and partner staff (news, product innovation, key messages, strategic discussions, trend discussion) (value communication)

55 30-second value elevator pitch by product and service (value-based marketing)

D. Example of value journal

Value Journal

Week: _____

Value Mindset Personal Goals:
1.
2.
3.
4.
5.

Positive Affirmation about Value:
1.
2.
3.
4.
5.

<Logo Here>

Daily Value Task Execution | Duration | Outcome
1.
2.
3.
4.
5.
6.
7.
8.
9.
10.

Personal Comments

E. Value mindset assessment

Attitude

	Rarely		Neutral		Always	Score
We are confident that we can accomplish great things in our organization	1	2	3	4	5	
We see the positive in people, situations, and events more than the negative	1	2	3	4	5	
We seek to improve by setting measurable and challenging goals	1	2	3	4	5	
We are well equipped to face any unforeseen issues and potential roadblocks	1	2	3	4	5	
					Sub-total	0

Action

	Rarely		Neutral		Always	Score
We have a clear list of daily actions we have to take to support value programs	1	2	3	4	5	
We are able to concretely apply what we learn in training and transform that in practical activities	1	2	3	4	5	
We have value tools that reinforce the need to practice our value programs on a daily basis	1	2	3	4	5	
We receive feedback and coaching on personal action plans to improve our performance with value programs	1	2	3	4	5	
					Sub-total	0

Ability

	Rarely		Neutral		Always	Score
We have received proper training in all relevant dimensions of value management	1	2	3	4	5	
We have been able to practice and experiment new tools, methods, and concepts prior to introducing them to market	1	2	3	4	5	
We have learned from best practices, value success stories, external benchmarks, and lessons learned	1	2	3	4	5	
We have access to value experts, coaches, additional training when we need reinforcement on key value concepts	1	2	3	4	5	
					Sub-total	0

Accountability

	Rarely		Neutral		Always	Score
We have a strong culture of effort and accountability in our organization	1	2	3	4	5	
We fully understand the consequences of not fully supporting value programs	1	2	3	4	5	
Compensation plans are designed to encourage efforts and improvements with value programs	1	2	3	4	5	
We understand that value programs requires everyone's involvement and we all support each other to succeed	1	2	3	4	5	
					Sub-total	0

Adaptability

	Rarely		Neutral		Always	Score
We adapt by smoothly juggling multiple demands and managing multiple projects	1	2	3	4	5	
We adapt quickly to shifting priorities and rapid change	1	2	3	4	5	
We adapt overall strategy, goals, or projects to fit the situation in front of us	1	2	3	4	5	
we adapt by applying standard procedures flexibly and being mindful of what works or does not	1	2	3	4	5	
					Sub-total	0

Alignment

	Rarely		Neutral		Always	Score
We have a clear understanding of the overarching corporate strategy	1	2	3	4	5	
All compensation plans are aligned with value and profit objectives	1	2	3	4	5	
Corporate priorities are integrated to achieve the same goals centered around value excellence	1	2	3	4	5	
Business unit & corporate managers work on integrative & aligned priorities	1	2	3	4	5	
					Sub-total	0

Value Mindset Assessment Score (out of 120 possible points) — **Total Score: 0**

Made in the USA
Columbia, SC
14 October 2017